Bahrmann/Links
The Fall of the Wall

Hannes Bahrmann
Christoph Links

The Fall of the Wall

The Path to German Reunification

Translated by Belinda Cooper

Ch.Links

Ch. Links Verlag, Berlin

This book is a short version of the German edition of »Chronik der Wende«, published in 1999 by Christoph Links Verlag – LinksDruck GmbH, Berlin.

Die Deutsche Bibliothek – CIP-Einheitsaufnahme

Bahrmann, Hannes:
The fall of the wall: the path to German reunification/Hannes Bahrmann; Christoph Links. Transl. by Belinda Cooper. – Short version of the German ed. of »Chronik der Wende«. – Berlin: Links, 1999
ISBN 3-86153-203-4

Zehdenicker Straße 1, D-10119 Berlin, Tel.: (49-30-)44 02 32-0
Internet: www.linksverlag.de
Jacket design: KahaneDesign, Berlin
Jacket photo: Eberhard Klöppel
Set by Susanne Heerdegen, Ch. Links Verlag
Printed in Germany by Friedrich Pustet, Regensburg
ISBN 3-86153-203-4

Introduction

The dramatic changes in East Germany in autumn of 1989 have been labeled many things in hindsight: awakening, radical reform, even revolution. But of all the scholarly definitions and literary descriptions, none has taken as firm a hold as the expression *Wende* – literally, a turn. It is not the most precise phrase, and its original meaning was quite different. It was first employed by Egon Krenz on October 18, 1989, following his election as the new Socialist Unity Party (SED) General Secretary, when he uncertainly addressed the public on East German television. In his view, the removal of Party leader and head of state Erich Honecker would initiate a »turn« in Party efforts to »retake the political and ideological offensive.« But the public interpreted the »turn« in its own way, taking the offensive itself. The rigged local elections of May 7, 1989 had been the last straw. At a time when rigid social conditions in the East Bloc had finally begun to relax, Gorbachev's Soviet Union was starting to reform and opposition candidates were campaigning in Poland, East German citizens were exhorted to provide a »unanimous show of support for the candidates of the National Front« – that is, to give their unchallenged blessing to the single SED-dominated list of candidates. But now, for the first time, citizens' groups and church organizations set out to observe the ballot counting, and they registered several more percentage points' worth of crossed-out names – that is, »no« votes – than the official figures announced by Election Chairman Egon Krenz.

The disinterest in reforms on the part of SED leaders, reinforced by East Germany's official support for the violent suppression of the democratic movement in China in early June, led to a mass exodus of East Germans to West Germany, which was in any case viewed by many as an attractive alternative. By autumn, tens of thousands had reached the West through the Hungarian border with Austria or the West German embassies in Prague, Warsaw and Budapest. Despite this »voting with their feet,« the doddering SED leadership, completely oblivious to reality, prepared once again to celebrate itself, choosing for the purpose East Germany's fortieth anniversary on October 7, 1989.

But the celebration turned into its opposite, and would mark the beginning of the end. In Leipzig, Dresden and Berlin, protests of as-yet unheard of magnitude took place and spread during the days that followed. In the process, they challenged the ruling party's right to continue acting in the name of the people. At the end of October, tens of thousands took to the streets shouting »We are the people« and demanding radical transformation of their society. They insisted that democratic freedoms had to become a permanent reality in Germany's east as well as its west, and they were no longer willing to be bought off with promises and a few concessions. The right to demonstrate, defiantly won in the streets, and the right to travel, which suddenly became the norm through the unexpected opening of the Wall on November 9, were followed by the rights of speech and assembly and the gradual disempowering of the ruling party and its »security organs.«

At no point did opposition groups make any attempt to take direct power. The majority were certain that government without their participation was no longer possible; they believed they needed only to push consistently for rapid, free elections. The continuing rallies, especially in the south of the country, were impressive proof of this. Thus, the second phase of restructuring was characterized above all by a debate over the modalities of the first free elections in the history of East Germany, a debate in which the West German parties would then set the tone. The clear vote on March 18, 1990 for the conservative »Alliance for Germany« and its program of rapid joinder with West Germany marked the end of the actual *Wende*. It was a true transfer of power, accomplished by peaceful means, and led to official unification on October 3, 1990.

Germany had never before experienced a similar successful popular uprising against an illegitimate ruler. Our aim has been to document this special process in all its facets.

Christoph Links/Hannes Bahrmann
Berlin, May 1999

October 1989

Saturday, October 7

Today East Germany turns 40. In East Berlin, the day begins with street cleaning: cleanup crews clear away the remains of last night's torchlight parade by the Free German Youth, at which a hundred thousand young people marched past Party leader and head of state Erich Honecker. At 10:00 a.m. a large military parade begins on Karl Marx Allee, despite objections from the Western allies. In the afternoon, all districts in the city hold street fairs. But little enthusiasm is evident; the country is experiencing an unprecedented degree of tension. Since September 10, thousands of people, many of them young, have been abandoning the country for the West, fleeing through Hungary or seeking refuge in West German consulates in Prague and Warsaw. The reasons are many: dissatisfaction with restrictions on travel, limited rights to free expression, lack of political freedom, the hypocrisy of the media, the shortage of consumer goods in comparison with the West, the deterioration of cities and factories. All this has caused disillusionment – and determination.

Around 5 p.m., several hundred young people gather on Alexanderplatz in East Berlin »to whistle at the elections*.« They protest the manipulation of the most recent local elections with a concert of whistles, then debate with onlookers and begin to chant slogans. In contrast to earlier rallies, with their choruses of »We want out!«, this time the defiant cry is »We're staying here!« – meaning that the problems that have accumulated cannot simply be pushed aside, but must be dealt with in the country itself.

The protesters move in the direction of the Palace of the Republic, where top state and Party officials are celebrating the country's anniversary with invited guests, including Soviet reformer Mikhail Gorbachev; the crowd, now grown to two or three thousand, chants »Gorbi, help us« and »We are the people!« But they are pushed back by police, and turn north toward the district of Prenzlauer Berg. There, in the Gethsemane Church (Gethsemanekirche), a vigil for political prisoners

* *In German, to »whistle at« (pfeifen auf) something implies contempt; one couldn't care less about it.*

has been going on since last week. When the demonstrators pass the offices of ADN, the state news agency, they yell »Liars! Liars!« and »Press freedom – freedom of opinion!« Police cars begin to arrive on the scene, and officers block off the side streets. There are scuffles and arrests, with police using their clubs. »No violence!« cries the crowd, surging forward. Fifteen hundred people finally reach the Gethsemane Church on Schönhauser Allee, as special units of the police and security officers hermetically seal the area. Toward midnight comes the order to attack; the same occurs in Leipzig, Dresden, Plauen, Jena, Magdeburg, Ilmenau, Arnstadt, Karl-Marx-Stadt and Potsdam, where other political demonstrations on this holiday are also broken up forcibly. The same evening, a Social Democratic Party (SDP) for East Germany is founded in the small town of Schwante, north of Berlin. The party demands an ecologically-oriented social market economy with democratic control of economic power, free labor unions with the right to strike, the right to travel and emigrate, and recognition of two German states.

Sunday, October 8

At Sunday mass, religious leaders call for calm and nonviolence. The dissident movement »New Forum,« founded a few weeks ago, distributes typed flyers exhorting, »Force is not a method of political debate. Do not let yourselves be provoked!«

More violent confrontations take place in Dresden. Mayor Wolfgang Berghofer attempts to begin a dialogue, meeting with a spontaneously formed citizens' committee called the »Group of Twenty«; but the police, following orders from the top, again employ force. Among those arrested is Michael Dulig, who describes what happened:

»We had to stand with our faces to the wall, legs spread and hands leaning diagonally against the wall. It's called the flyer's position. In this position, we were subjected to a body search and had our IDs and belts taken from us. An officer in battle dress, probably the operation chief, informed us that we were in a militarily-secured building. If we attempted to escape, weapons would be used. Around 10:30 p.m., correction officer trainees in battle dress stormed the garage, yelling. They beat us in the back and neck with clubs, grabbed those standing farthest back and brutally shoved them into the position required. They beat them with clubs or kicked them between the legs until they had spread their legs wide enough. Those who didn't react immediately or who complained were shouted at, brutally dragged out of the garage, and thrown against the gates ...«

On the evening of October 8, violent scenes also play out around Gethsemane Church in East Berlin. Following a prayer service, police units surround the crowd leaving the church and demand that all 3,000 pass individually through a checkpoint. But the group stays together and, lit candles in hand, begins a sitdown strike. At that, the police forcibly clear the area. The cries of the victims mingle with the midnight tocsin from the church. Violence escalates uncontrollably.

Monday, October 9

In Leipzig, the situation takes a dangerous turn before the weekly Monday demonstration by opposition groups. It becomes known that medical personnel have been called in for night duty, entire hospital wards cleared and additional blood reserves prepared. People expect the worst this evening. The Tienanmen Square syndrome is in the air; it is no longer possible to rule out a violent response on the Chinese model, with many injured and perhaps killed. In this situation, prominent artists, including the Chief Conductor of the Gewandhaus Orchestra, Kurt Masur, a pastor and three district Socialist Unity Party [SED] Secretaries meet to begin an initiative for de-escalation. In the afternoon, their joint statement is read out on local radio: »We are distressed by the developments in our city and are seeking a solution. We all need a free exchange of opinions about how to develop socialism in our country ...We urge you to remain calm so that a peaceful dialogue will be possible.«

In the evening, Leipzig witnesses the largest protest demonstration in East Germany since the uprising of June 17, 1953: seventy thousand people march through the city center. The police no longer stand a chance, and they retreat in face of this overwhelming mass. Again and again, the decisive cry echoes: »We are the people!« It tells those in power that they have forfeited the right to act in the name of the people.

Tuesday, October 10

Many breath a sigh of relief; in most cities, the night has passed peacefully. Only the industrial city of Halle has again seen brutal police attacks on demonstrators. In East Berlin, though, security forces were withdrawn, so that a quiet rally around the Gesthemane Church breaks up on its own in the early morning hours. Throughout the night, candles burn in many windows in the neighborhood as a token of solidarity.

Behind the scenes, the power struggle escalates. The SED Politburo, the actual center of power in the country, meets today in plenary session. But there is no clear majority for reform as yet.

While the political leadership cannot agree and remains largely paralyzed, the demands of various grass-roots groups gain in force and variety. Along with New Forum's call for a dialogue on democratizing society, the platform of the newly-founded SDP for reforming East Germany and the demands of the citizens' group Democracy Now (DJ)are distributed in churches and factories. The latter declares, »We want the socialist revolution, which never got past nationalization, to be carried on and given a perspective for the future. Instead of a custodial, Party-dominated state that has raised itself to the status of principal and schoolmaster over the people, with no social mandate, we want a state based on a fundamental social consensus that is accountable to society and thus becomes a public concern of mature citizens.«

Wednesday, October 11

The Politburo continues to meet, but has reached no decisions. In a final declaration, it again denies the need to democratize society and labels the past days' demonstrators »irresponsible disturbers of peace and order.« In a BBC interview, Markus Wolf, retired general of the Ministry for State Security, former espionage chief and advocate of the Gorbachev line in the East German leadership, says the changes in East Germany are too little and too slow, and adds that this is contributing to a sense of hopelessness among some segments of the population. At the orders of the SED leadership, all broadcasts by the West Berlin radio station *Hundert,6* in which the words East Germany appear are disrupted by heavy static. Obviously lacking arguments and wishing to conceal their own defensive political posture, these leaders fall back on Cold War methods.

Thursday, October 12

In an attempt to stop the stream of emigrants to West German consulates in Prague, or from Hungary to Austria, the Ministry of the Interior announces that only retirees and invalids may apply to travel to Czechoslovakia for the present. These are the same people who are allowed to travel to the West under current law. Since visa-free travel to Poland was suspended on October 30, 1980, Czechoslovakia has been the only country to which East Germans could travel without permission and using only their identity cards. Nine million East Germans visited this neighboring country in 1988 alone. Travel documents are necessary for all other socialist countries, and they require application to the police weeks in advance. Since 1980, travel to Poland has also required an invitation.

Grass-roots demands for change become louder. For example, New Forum demands (1) official recognition of all grass-roots groups, parties and initiatives working for democratization of society; (2) access to the mass media; (3) press freedom and the elimination of censorship; (4) freedom of assembly and the right to demonstrate.

Friday, October 13

In the morning, the SED leadership, represented by Erich Honecker and his two closest advisors, Central Committee Secretaries Günter Mittag and Joachim Herrmann, meets in East Berlin with the chairmen of the four parties that, together with the SED, officially comprise the parliament's »democratic bloc.« Honecker proposes that socialism in East Germany be »constantly improved by thoroughgoing change and reform,« but at the same time makes it clear that the current model of sole SED leadership will be retained.

In the afternoon, the Prosecutor General's office announces that, with the exception of eleven people under investigation for acts of violence, all arrested demonstrators have been released. Prominent East Berlin lawyer Wolfgang Vogel, a confidant of Honecker who has dealt with difficult inter-German humanitarian cases, calls for the release of all East Germans arrested for attempting to leave the country and in connection with the recent demonstrations.

Saturday, October 14

In the morning, the 50,000th East Germany refugee since the opening of the Hungarian border arrives in West Germany. The radio station Sender Freies Berlin (Radio Free Berlin) broadcasts a portrait of a couple who fled from East to West Berlin via Hungary. The young woman is filmed looking for a job. Already, of the 84,000 unemployed in the western part of the city, every tenth person is an East German immigrant.

Some 120 members of New Forum, whose founding statement has now been signed by over 25,000 people, meet in East Berlin for their first coordination meeting. There, it is announced that the mayor of Karl-Marx-Stadt has offered to enter into a dialogue with representatives of New Forum. Official contact has also taken place in Leipzig and Potsdam. However, representatives in Halle have encountered difficulties, with some arrested by the police in recent days. The members foresee the movement spreading according to a grass-roots principle. They plan to form a coordinating committee and elect a speakers' council made up of representatives from the regional centers.

Unlike the SDP, which emerged from the beginning with an almost complete structure and platform, the citizens' movement Democracy Now, with 1,000 members at this point, takes a similar approach to that of New Forum. »We propose that you seek connections with like-minded groups in your neighborhood. Organize meetings in districts and counties. Elect spokeswomen and spokesmen. Send representatives to national events,« says one of their flyers.

Sunday, October 15

In Berlin, the ongoing vigils and prayer services are showing signs of success: the demonstrators arrested on October 7 and 8 are freed. But the vigils continue. Participants demand an investigation of police abuses and punishment of those responsible.

The East Berlin initiative Democratic Awakening meets today. The group formed over the summer out of church-based groups; its best-known member so far is Rainer Eppelmann, pastor of Berlin's Samaritan Church (Samariterkirche). In an open letter to East Berlin Mayor Erhard Krack, the group calls for creation of an independent investigatory commission to look into the rights violations on October 7 and 8. Violence and intimidation, they say, cannot be suitable conditions for democratic dialogue.

In the evening, a »Concert against Violence« takes place in East Berlin's Redeemer Church (Erlöserkirche). Singers and writers call for fundamental reforms. Enormous applause breaks out when writer and songwriter Gerhard Schöne announces that, of the 20,000 marks he received as part of the East German National Prize he was awarded on October 7, he is giving half to a church development aid group and half to the arrestees.

Monday, October 16

Harry Tisch, head of the FDGB, the unified official trade union, admits after discussions with workers, that »the mood among workers has changed.« Instead of agreement with SED policies, he is treated to harsh criticism. Nevertheless, he clings to the old line. In his opinion, East Germany needs no new democratic fora, as it already has all necessary structures. To a journalist's question whether reports of power struggles within the SED Politburo are true, Tisch, who has belonged to the body since 1975, responds, »Numerous Western media are specialists in reading coffee grounds. They spread lies, falsify information, manipulate half-truths. They blend fact and fantasy to fit their anti-Communist concept, now more than ever.« He has nothing else to say about the current situation.

Outside the country, the situation is viewed more soberly and thus more realistically. Vyacheslav Dachichev, one of Mikhail Gorbachev's foreign policy advisors, says in a talk with the *Frankfurter Rundschau* newspaper, »The mood among the East German population reflects conditions in the country. If the leadership does not notice this, it can lead to very dangerous discrepancies between the thinking of the government and of the public ...East Germany's entire economic and political system is based on the old Stalinist concept of administrative socialism.«

In the evening, more people take to the streets than ever before: 120,000 in Leipzig alone, 10,000 each in Dresden and Magdeburg, 5,000 in Halle and 3,000 in East Berlin. Their demands are similar: recognition of New Forum, free elections, freedom of the press and of opinion, elimination of the visa requirement for travel to Czechoslovakia and complete freedom to travel.

Tuesday, October 17

In East Berlin, more than 4,000 students at Humboldt University discuss overdue reforms. Their demands include independent student representatives, an uncensored student newspaper, and unrestricted access to all library materials and to photocopiers.

Workers at the Wilhelm Pieck Appliance and Regulator Factory in Teltow, south of Berlin, leave the FDGB to form an independent enterprise group called *Reform*. They call for the creation of independent trade unions.

Wednesday, October 18

In the morning, Manfred von Ardenne, a well-known Dresden scientist, says he has the impression that the SED leadership has not yet grasped the seriousness of the situation and complains that there have been no »significant deeds and changes.« He is articulating the feeling of a majority of the population.

In the afternoon comes sensational news: Erich Honecker has resigned. At his suggestion, Egon Krenz is elected as the new General Secretary of the SED Central Committee. The announcement about the Central Committee meeting continues with the news that Politburo members and Central Committee Secretaries Günter Mittag (economy) and Joachim Herrmann (media) have been removed from their posts.

Thus the actual power center around Erich Honecker has been destroyed, bringing an epoch in East German history to an end. Over the years, these three men amassed a degree of power bordering on classical absolutism. Honecker's closest confidant, Günter Mittag, conducted and oversaw 22 economic ministries, 224 combines and 3,526 industrial enterprises. Joachim Herrmann presided over a similar empire: not only was he responsible for all SED and related media, he also, through a coordinating body – the Council of Ministers' press office – controlled the news agencies, radio, television and all other newspapers and magazines. Every evening, Herrmann called editors to tell them how the next day's newspapers were to look, how large Honecker's page-one photo had to be, and where an unavoidable unpleasant report should be hidden in the inside pages.

In the evening, East German television broadcasts Egon Krenz's first public pronouncement in his new capacity. Krenz, former head of the

Free German Youth (FDJ), the central youth organization, and most recently responsible for security and cadre issues in the SED Central Committee, shows little understanding of public expectations. However, for the first time he admits errors on the part of the political leadership: »It is clear that in recent months we did not judge the nature of developments in our country realistically enough and failed to draw the right conclusions in time.« He speaks nebulously of wanting to introduce a »turn« (*Wende*) in East Germany.

Thursday, October 19

Hans Modrow, SED district chief in Dresden, speaks out publicly, calling for dialogue among all sectors in East Germany. He says the political situation requires thoroughgoing changes, adding, »In this comprehensive renewal, the experience of the Soviet Union should also be utilized.« The dialogue that has begun should not stop at differences of opinion, Modrow maintains, but must contribute to a decision-making process and lead to decisions. Thus, he takes the side of forces within the SED that are urging rapid reform à la Gorbachev.

The outflow of refugees that helped trigger the radical change in leadership remains one of the main themes of public discussion. Economist Peter Thal calculates the following in the newspaper Junge Welt: Given a national income of 268.4 billion marks and a current workforce of 8.6 million, every ten thousand emigrants means a loss of 0.12 percent of national income, or 330 million marks. Since the emigrants are mostly young people, East Germany is losing some ten billion marks per ten thousand emigrants, projected onto the coming year. In his opinion, regulations must therefore be adopted immediately to permit visits to the West.

In the evening, politicians, scholars and journalists discuss the situation on television. All voice the hope that a travel law promised by the Council of Ministers will lead to a passport for every citizen and the opportunity for unrestricted travel.

On the streets, the protests continue. In Zittau, in the south, 20,000 people take part in a New Forum event. The City Council permits it to be broadcast by loudspeaker from inside St. John's Church (Johanniskirche) so the thousands gathered outside can hear it – a procedure that would have been unthinkable only a few days ago.

In Halle, on the other hand, representatives of New Forum are arrested while attempting to organize a public event. Demonstrations for serious reforms take place in Rostock (10,000 participants), Zeulenroda (3,000), Stendal (500) and Erfurt (300).

Friday, October 20

For the first time, the East German government offers every citizen who has gone to the West the chance to return. »Unless there are convincing reasons not to, we will help those wishing to return as far as possible to reestablish themselves in the land of their birth,« announces Foreign Ministry spokesman Wolfgang Meyer. At the same time, appealing to people still wishing to leave the country, he warns, »No one should make decisions or take hasty actions that he might regret later on.«

The government instructs the Minister of the Interior to draft a travel law. The Minister of Justice is to present, as soon as possible, a plan for legal change in the coming year.

Postal Minister Rudolf Schulze announces that the Soviet monthly *Sputnik* can once again be distributed. The ban on *Sputnik* a year ago resulted in public protests by tens of thousands of East Germans. The ban – justified on November 25, 1988 in the Party daily *Neues Deutschland* with the explanation that the journal did not contribute to German-Soviet friendship, but instead published »distorted historical articles« – had finally brought into the open the conflict between the East German leadership and Mikhail Gorbachev's policies. The East German media had already been strictly forbidden by the SED Central Committee Department of Agitation from using the words *glasnost* and *perestroika*.

In the evening, 50,000 people march through the center of Dresden demanding free elections. In Halle, where violent confrontations have taken place with the powers-that-be in recent days, there is still no apparent willingness to engage in dialogue. In the city's St. George's Church (Georgenkirche), participants in a vigil demand talks with municipal leaders. Surprisingly, this evening the young people's TV program *Elf 99*, on East German television, reports on the behavior of the security forces around the church. For the first time, reporters interview participants in the vigil and members of the opposition. Demonstrations take place in Gotha (6,000), Karl-Marx-Stadt (5,000), Klingenthal (2,000) and numerous other small towns in the south.

Saturday, October 21

In East Berlin, protesters form a human chain through the center of the city, demanding the release of everyone arrested on October 7 and 8 and an end to legal proceedings against nonviolent demonstrators throughout the country.

SED Politburo member Günter Schabowski and East Berlin Mayor Erhard Krack take part in a discussion with demonstrators outside the People's Chamber (parliament). The debate turns on press freedom, freedom of speech and assembly, travel opportunities and forms of dialogue between citizens and state leaders.

This weekend, the Liberal Democratic Party (LDPD), until now closely tied to the SED, releases a statement in which it calls on the SED not only to speak with individual members of New Forum, but also to grant this democratic movement official recognition. The Liberal Democrats say they are prepared to accept members of New Forum into their own ranks and »allow them to campaign on their own list.« New Forum thanks them for this public support, but emphasizes its desire to remain independent. Some members even criticize what they call inappropriate attempts at cooptation employed by the various parties of the »democratic bloc« to better their own reputations.

Demonstrations continue throughout the country. In Plauen, 35,000 people take part in the largest demonstration yet in this industrial town of 80,000 in the Karl-Marx-Stadt district, near the West German border. Their demands include immediate democratization of society, free elections, recognition of New Forum, the right to travel freely, and, for the first time, German unification. A rally of 10,000 in the city on October 7 was broken up violently by the People's Police; since then, rallies have been held every Saturday. Demonstrations also take place in Rostock, Potsdam, Dresden, Jena and Karl-Marx-Stadt.

Sunday, October 22

Five hundred Leipzig residents meet this morning in the Gewandhaus concert hall to initiate a broad public debate. Conductor Kurt Masur opens the discussion by saying, »What we are able to resolve here could point the way for the entire Republic.« He asks for proposals on how the »Leipzig model« could serve as an example for others. The debate lasts several hours; the themes it outlines – reformation of political relationships, educational reform, ecology, and city planning – will be taken up later by commissions, with the participation of all interested parties, in order to provide concrete recommendations. It is agreed that from now on, Leipzigers will meet every Sunday for a »dialogue on Karl Marx Square.«

A group called the »United Left« announces a two-day meeting in East Berlin at the end of November at which they will make their program public for the first time. In a position paper, they make it clear that they oppose the dictatorial state, but not the idea of socialism; they expressly advocate retention of social ownership of the means of production, except that such property must be changed, through workers' councils, into the direct property of the workers. They also believe an alternative must be found to party-centered parliamentarism. This distinguishes the group from the recently founded East German Social Democratic Party (SDP) and the Democratic Awakening movement, both of which advocate a controlled market economy and forms of parliamentary democracy.

Monday, October 23

Over 300,000 demonstrators take part in the weekly Leipzig demonstration, making it the largest protest in the history of East Germany. Banners read »Power to the People« and call for democratic elections and independent labor unions.

In an East Berlin church, representatives of several citizens' initiatives, including New Forum, submit a one-hundred-page report containing eye-witness and factual accounts of the violent police actions of October 7 and 8. The First Vice-Prosecutor General of East Berlin, Klaus Voss, promises that »all related charges, facts and petitions will be investigated completely and without prejudice.« Consistory President Manfred Stolpe of the Protestant Church demands »the courage to face the truth, even when it hurts.«

The strangest demonstration of recent days takes place in Schwerin. Attempting to circumvent a call by New Forum for a protest against the planned multiple election of Egon Krenz to the offices of Party chief and head of state, the district SED leadership mobilizes its own membership for a rally in the same place in favor of the *Wende*. There they take over the microphones of the public debate, and the 40,000 people in attendance are treated to an alternating hail of completely contradictory viewpoints. The crowd is split, clapping and whistling by turns throughout the event.

Tuesday, October 24

Despite many protests, SED chief Egon Krenz this morning is elected by the People's Chamber to the positions of both Chairman of the Council of State and Chairman of the National Defense Council. The former holder of these offices, Erich Honecker, is first removed from these functions; however, due to ill health, he does not take part in the proceedings. For the first time in the parliament's forty-year history, the vote for a head of state is not unanimous; 26 deputies vote against and 26 abstain. Horst Sindermann, President of the People's Chamber, has obvious difficulty dealing with this new practice. He miscounts, turns to his neighbor for help, and then promises, »I will not falsify the result!«

A few hours later, 12,000 people demonstrate in East Berlin against Krenz's election. The demonstrators place candles in front of the Council of State building, which is surrounded and blocked off by a chain of uniformed members of the Ministry for State Security.

Krenz resembles former General Secretary Erich Honecker in many ways, including his career path. In 1971 he took over leadership of the Pioneer youth organization; three years later he became First Secretary of the Central Council of the FDJ youth association, a position he – like Honecker – held for nine years. In 1983 he became a member of the SED Politburo, and a year later was named one of Honecker's deputies in the office of Chairman of the Council of State. Since then, Krenz has been considered the »crown prince.«

Protests take place again in ten towns, most of them – except for Anklam and Demmin in the north – in the south: Dresden, Meissen, Nordhausen, Wernigerode, Aschersleben.

Wednesday, October 25

Throughout the country, people are finding their voices. In Neubrandenburg, in the northeast, some 20,000 people gather for a »march of hope« following a prayer service for peace at St. John's Church

(Johanniskirche). The same occurs in Halberstadt, where 10,000 people demonstrate today, and in Jena, where the chant on the street is »Democracy – now or never!« Greifswald residents hold a major rally for more democracy.

On the other hand, SED Politburo member Günter Schabowski declares on West German television this evening that East Germany already possesses all the essential elements of a socialist state based in the rule of law. According to him, these must simply be perfected through the Wende process. He rejects the idea of a »dialogue in the streets.«

Thursday, October 26

In the morning, East Berlin SED chief Schabowski receives the initiators of New Forum, Bärbel Bohley and Professor Jens Reich, in his office. This is the first official meeting between a senior functionary and representatives of a reform group.

The first telephone conversation between Egon Krenz and Chancellor Helmut Kohl brings no relief for the East German leadership. The conversation is a more or less non-committal one about economic issues. In the twenty-minute call, Krenz makes it clear that East Germany will remain a socialist country despite the reforms and he asks Kohl to respect East German citizenship. No meeting of minds is achieved.

Hundreds of thousands gather this evening in Dresden, Rostock, Erfurt, Gera, and Frankfurt/Oder for more rallies, intensifying their demands for elimination of the SED's monopoly of power, free elections, and unlimited democratic rights.

A hundred thousand people come together in Dresden for talks with Mayor Berghofer and district party boss Hans Modrow. Modrow declares, »What has begun will trigger revolutionary change in East Germany!« Berghofer provides information on the results of an extraordinary meeting of the City Council that took place during the day. There, working groups were formed in which interested citizens – including representatives of the »Group of 20« opposition group – could assist in policymaking for a specified period. Dr. Frank Tellkamp of New Forum confirms in his presentation that 3.5 million people have left the country in the last 40 years. He says it is high time to introduce thoroughgoing reform of the economy, with an orientation toward the market and competition, reform of the social system – including surrender of the SED's monopoly of power – free elections and freedom to travel.

Friday, October 27

The Council of State adopts an amnesty for all East German citizens who have left the country illegally. It provides that anyone arrested for trying to »flee the Republic« will be freed within three days and all charges based on this crime dropped. The amnesty also applies to people arrested at prohibited demonstrations.

The Council of Ministers rescinds the restrictions on travel to Czechoslovakia imposed on October 12. All East German citizens may now travel to their southeastern neighbor without a visa or passport. This also means that the stream of thousands of people leaving the country daily for West Germany via Czechoslovakia and Austria can swell again.

However, open borders and a universal right to travel are still being ruled out. In an interview with East German television, Prosecutor General Horst Wendland expressly rejects the elimination of the crime of »illegal border crossing.« He says that the border between East and West Germany separates »two incompatible systems« and must therefore be guarded reliably.

Protests begin to grow in small and medium-sized towns. This evening they are held in over 30 places, including Güstrow (20,000), Dessau (15,000), Saalfeld (10,000), Olbernhau (4,000), Parchim (4,000), Lauchhammer (3,500), and Großräschen (1,500).

Saturday, October 28

In Berlin, the Initiative for Peace and Human Rights (IFM), founded in 1985 as one of the first independent dissident groups in the country and home of the initiators of New Forum, officially constitutes itself a »political association.» It calls for external and internal disarmament and demilitarization, the right to refuse military service, rule of law and the separation of Party, state and society. Numerous regional groups subsequently form and cooperate to network the opposition movement.

The search for a realignment of their political place in a turbulently changing society also grips traditional SED allies. Today, the Christian Democratic Union (CDU) in East Germany publishes a statement of principles in its party organ *Neue Zeit*, in which it defines itself as an independent party. In an eight-point program, it demands a thorough change in public life that puts ethical values first and is characterized by vital democracy, strict rule of law, and realistic media.

In Leipzig, Erfurt and Jena, contentious debates take place with local SED representatives. Thirty thousand people gather in front of the City Hall in Plauen and demand official recognition of New Forum. In Greiz, 6,000 people take part in the first permitted opposition rally. Banners read »No more talking – we want action.« In Jena, discussions focus on environmental protection and local issues.

In the evening, prominent authors, artists and scholars gather for a protest in East Berlin's Redeemer Church (Erlöserkirche). They include Christa Wolf, Christoph Hein, Stefan Heym, Heiner Müller, Stephan Hermlin, Günther de Bruyn and Helga Königsdorf. A young woman who spent several days in investigative detention for putting up posters calling for social renewal reports on unbelievable violence and the subtle mechanisms of intimidation. In addition to photos and fingerprints, the security forces also took »smell samples« from her and her 12-year-old sister – to help the bloodhounds find them later, they were told.

At the same time, a reading takes place in the Deutsches Theater of the memoirs of Walter Janka. The former director of the *Aufbau* publishing house was arrested in 1956 on trumped-up charges (the attempted overthrow of the Ulbricht government) and sentenced to five years' imprisonment. This is Janka's first major public appearance, and he offers thanks for this moral rehabilitation, making the evening simultaneously a political rally for the rehabilitation of all victims of Stalinism.

Sunday, October 29

»Open Doors – Open Words« is the slogan of the first mass event in East Berlin at which top politicians engage in discussion with the public. The auditorium in the East Berlin City Hall in which it is supposed to be held proves far too small, as 20,000 people show up. The debate is moved outdoors and turns into a rally. It begins with a moment of silence; one speaker explains, »We must remember those who paid with their lives for attempting to solve their problem individually, dying in minefields or by spring guns or in the waters of the Spree river for their desire to see the world just once.« In the course of a six-hour discussion, the »protective and security organs« are harshly criticized – specifically the Ministry for State Security, whose dissolution is demanded publicly for the first time. Shrill whistling breaks out when, after repeated demands, police chief Rausch finally apologizes for the abuses on October 7 and 8. In contrast, there is stormy applause for the suggestions that the gated Politburo community in Wandlitz, near East Berlin, be turned into a home for handicapped children and that privileges for state and Party leaders be entirely eliminated.

Similar demands are made in public debates in Karl-Marx-Stadt and Leipzig. »The patient, Leipzig, is ill, and prescriptions no longer do any good. We need radical surgery,« is the tenor of a seven-and-a-half-hour discussion in the Leipzig Gewandhaus concert hall. Participants call for more attention to their region, the largest area of industrial concentration in East Germany.

Demonstrations are held in many other cities following Sunday services: in Ueckermünde on the Ostseehaff, Rostock, and Bad Salzungen in Thuringia. Their demands, under the banner »We are the People,« include legalization of New Forum, creation of civil alternatives to military service, and implementation of freedom of the press.

Monday, October 30

At an assembly of delegates in East Berlin, Democratic Awakening decides to change itself from a movement to a political party by May 1, 1990 at the latest. The 200 delegates elect Wolfgang Schnur, a lawyer from Rostock, their chairman, and Pastor Reiner Eppelmann is appointed press spokesperson. In a preliminary statement of principles, the emerging party calls for control of the state by society, encouragement of small and middle-sized industry, application of market economy principles, ecological restructuring of industrial society and an »active coming together of the two German states.«

Ecological problems have meanwhile become an issue at almost every public event. The extreme environmental pollution in East Germany and the government's coverup of data on the subject triggers strong protest, especially in the densely industrialized regions of the country. As a result of public pressure, the city government of Karl-Marx-Stadt promises to release all environmental data. In addition, an anti-smog regulation for all large cities is taken under consideration. The newspaper *Der Morgen* reports that emissions of nearly five million tons of sulphur dioxide and close to a million tons of nitrogen oxides were measured throughout the country in 1987, but these data were never released to the public.

Demonstrations are held all over the country this Monday evening. In Leipzig, some 250,000 people take to the streets once again. The demonstration's focus is a call for the SED to give up its monopoly of power. Protesters chant »Stasi* to the factories« and »Free elections, true numbers.« Fifty thousand residents of Halle call for consistent environmental protection in the most highly polluted industrial region of East Germany, carrying banners proclaiming »Let's see actions, we'll be there.« In Schwerin, 40,000 demand the elimination of privileges, and equality for all political parties. Twenty thousand demonstrate in Karl-Marx-Stadt for »Democracy – now!« and the adoption of a civil alternative to military service. In Pößneck, Thuringia, 5,000 people participate in a silent march through the town. Twenty thousand demonstrate in Cottbus.

Tuesday, October 31

The Ministry of Public Education announces that four students expelled from East Berlin's Carl von Ossietzky school in October 1988 may continue their education. The four had questioned, on a student bulletin board, whether a military parade was appropriate on the anniversary of the founding of the Republic, given the general efforts toward disarmament. Their expulsion had been ordered from the top, and they had stood as a symbol of the doctrinaire policies of Education Minister Margot Honecker, wife of Erich Honecker.

The Ministry of the Interior announces that it is seriously considering official recognition of the New Forum citizens' initiative. On September 22, it had refused to legalize the movement, saying it represented a platform »hostile to the state« and was attempting to conceal its true intentions from the public.

* *Abbreviation for »State Security«*

FDGB Chairman Harry Tisch, who has been strongly criticized in recent days by various district committees and unions, now declares he is in fact willing to step down.

In the evening, a large demonstration takes place in Wittenberg, birthplace of the church reformer Martin Luther. The protesters nail their demands, in the form of seven theses, to the doors of the City Hall.

November 1989

Wednesday, November 1

Egon Krenz holds a press conference in Moscow at the close of two days of consultations with the Soviet leadership. He once again underlines the SED's claim to monopoly power, saying the party strives for »socialist pluralism« under SED leadership. He claims that the changes so far have been »the result of the work of the Politburo and the Central Committee« of the SED and not a reaction to pressure from the street. In response to questioning at the West German border, Krenz maintains that the reasons for the erection of the Berlin Wall remain and calls the idea of its elimination unrealistic.

In the evening, tens of thousands take advantage of their newly-won rights as mass demonstrations take place in Neubrandenburg, Frankfurt (Oder), Freital and Ilmenau. Participants demand the right to travel, perceptible democratic changes, and a clear distancing from the Stalinist past.

Thursday, November 2

It is a day of resignations. FDGB Chairman Harry Tisch does what union members have been demanding for some time and what he himself has already announced. The succession is symptomatic of the times; his office is filled by 55-year-old Annelis Kimmel, who has made a career as a typical functionary. This entails learning a profession or studying a subject in which one will never actually work, in her case mechanical engineering. Immediately after finishing her education she took up a party function, then was delegated to the Party college, where she earned a degree as a social scientist. In 1979, she became head of the East Berlin district board of the FDGB and a member of the FDGB Presidium and the SED district leadership in East Berlin. In 1981 she was elected to the People's Chamber, not as an SED deputy but as a member of the FDGB parliamentary group.

The most senior SED district secretary, Hans Albrecht in Suhl, also steps down as charges of corruption grow. His counterpart in Gera, Herbert Ziegenhahn, does the same. Two top politicians in the blo parties accept the consequences of former involvements: The Chairmen of the National Democratic Party (NDPD), Heinrich Homann, and the Christian Democratic Union (CDU), Gerald Götting, take their leave. The resignation of the SED government of Prime Minister Willi Stoph and of the People's Chamber Presidium are also demanded. This is urged in particular by the Liberal Democrats, who propose their Chairman Manfred Gerlach as parliamentary president.

Lieutenant General Willy Nyffenegger, police chief of the Dresden district, tells the *Sächsische Zeitung* newspaper that the People's Police has learned from past violent conflicts and will work in the future for political solutions and fruitful dialogue. He says the police will support rallies and public discussions by providing sound equipment, and maintains that they have become more mature over the past weeks.

Demonstrations take place in the evening throughout the country. In Erfurt, 30,000 people take to the streets to demand radical reform; 15,000 protest in Guben against the slow pace of reform, and 10,000 demonstrate in Gera and in Halle.

Friday, November 3

Responding to harsh criticism, Leipzig's mayor Bernd Seidel steps down. He had long refused to engage in serious dialogue with the public.

The SED newspaper *Neues Deutschland* apologizes to readers for a report on September 21, 1989, in which a cook for the sleeping-car company Mitropa claimed he had been drugged in Budapest with a menthol cigarette, kidnapped and taken to West Germany via Austria. The report was apparently intended to create the impression that East Germans were not leaving the country out of disappointment and anger, but instead being kidnapped by gangs. However, research has shown that the incident never actually happened.

Some annoyances that have been taboo for years are now openly discussed. Postal Minister Rudolph Schulze admits that it will take years to grant the roughly one million pending applications for telephone connections. He says he receives 100,000 petitions a year on the subject, and estimates it would take an investment of some nine billion marks to satisfy the demand for telephones.

In the evening, Egon Krenz, the head of state and Party chief, unexpectedly addresses the public in an announcement broadcast over television and radio. It is only a few hours before a major demonstration in East Berlin that theater people and artists have been preparing for weeks, and which has, for the first time, been officially permitted. Hundreds of thousands are expected, and the pressure on the leadership is increasing perceptibly. To anticipate some of the protests, Krenz announces far-reaching reforms and the resignation of leading politicians. He promises the resignation of SED Politburo members Herrmann Axen (Central Committee Secretary of Foreign Affairs), Kurt Hager (Central Committee Secretary of Science and Culture), Erich Mielke (Minister for State Security), Erich Mückenberger (Chief of the Party Control Commission), and Alfred Neumann (Vice Premier). The program announced by Krenz includes creation of a constitutional court, administrative reforms, introduction of a civil alternative to military service, term limits on elected functions, fundamental economic reform, internal democratization of the Party and comprehensive changes in educational policy. »We take the people's dissatisfaction very seriously,« he says. »A great deal of impatience is currently in play. This is understandable and can even be useful, but it also brings dangers. It is not possible, in a few weeks, not to mention a few days, to correct developments that have built up over the years into a tangle of serious contradictions and crisis phenomena. Rash, hasty action will ultimately be more damaging than useful.«

Then, in the evening, the news brings cause to rejoice: all of the 4,500 East German citizens who have sought refuge in the West German embassy in Prague are free to go to West Germany with no formalities. This creates a precedent, and the same evening, thousands stream into Czechoslovakia to join the move in the direction of Bavaria.

Saturday, November 4

The center of East Berlin has been entirely filled with demonstrators since the early morning. Traffic has come to a complete standstill. Actors wearing green and yellow sashes bearing the slogan »No Violence« are on hand to keep order, and are accepted goodnaturedly by everyone. A security partnership with the People's Police has been established. There are almost no uniforms in sight, not even in front of the People's Chamber and the Council of State building, which in

November 4: Nearly one million people gather for the largest protest demonstration in East German history. They demand freedom of assembly, press freedom and freedom of opinion.
(photo by Eberhard Klöppel)

the course of five hours will see hundreds of thousands file past, demanding freedom of press and assembly and radical reform. According to official estimates, more than half a million people take part in this, the largest protest demonstration in East German history. It concludes with a rally on Alexanderplatz that opens with actor Ulrich Mühe expressing what everyone is feeling: »It was just wonderful.« East Berlin has never witnessed so much shared determination and imaginative spontaneity, in such a radical yet calm atmosphere. Author Christa Wolf points out that the revolutionary movement has also liberated speech: »What was so difficult to articulate before suddenly rolls freely from our tongues. We are amazed at what we have obviously been thinking for so long, and what we now call out to each other, ›Democracy – now or never!‹, by which we mean power to the people.«

Even though the difficult phase of restructuring still lies ahead, all agree on this day that East Germany has changed more in the past four weeks than in all the previous four decades. November 4 becomes a milestone. The SED leadership can no longer ignore the demands of the masses; there is no going back to old methods of rule.

Sunday, November 5

In Halle, the central board of the Monuments Preservation Society of the East German *Kulturbund*, meeting to consider urgent measures to save historic city centers threatened with deterioration, demands harsh sanctions against unjustified demolitions. The society explains that the orientation in recent years toward industrial housing construction using prefabricated concrete slabs has led to housing projects on the outskirts of cities that are out of keeping with the landscape, while architecturally valuable city centers have fallen to pieces. There has been growing protest against this, and practical proposals are required in response.

In the evening, an »Initiative for the Establishment of an Ecological Green Party« forms in East Berlin's Confessional Church (Bekenntniskirche). The initiative issues a statement that reads, »The reorganization of our ruined environment is of decisive importance in renewing our society. But it is not only our environment that is already contaminated; to a much greater degree, so is our awareness, especially by the Utopia that ever-increasing prosperity and – as a condition

– continuous economic growth have been made the goal of social development.« It added that this is leading instead to the destruction of Earth's ecological system.

Monday, November 6

The draft of a new travel law is published in the media and meets with universal disapproval. People are annoyed by provisions such as long processing periods, the need to constantly apply for new exit visas, and the government's right to refuse to permit travel. The provision that »approval of private travel does not provide grounds for a right to the acquisition of means of payment for the trip« also triggers protest; East German currency is not convertible, so travelers to the West would find themselves with no money. There is demand for an uncomplicated, easily administered regulation.

In Dresden, the Council of Ministers decision not to build a planned silicon plant in the Gittersee area is made public. Citizens' groups have been fighting the project for months because of its feared hazardous effects on the environment. In the evening, the city experiences its largest demonstration to date. SED district chief Hans Modrow and Mayor Wolfgang Berghofer march at the head of the roughly 100,000 participants.

In Halle, too, 60,000 people demonstrate. In front of the SED district offices, they demand the resignation of district chief Hans-Joachim Böhme, also a Politburo member. In Karl-Marx-Stadt, Mayor Eberhard Langner meets with citizens for the third time this week and, to the applause of the 50,000 assembled, announces that he has already involved representatives of New Forum in municipal politics, without waiting for instructions »from above.«

At the by-now traditional Monday demonstration in Leipzig, held in the rain for the first time, the mood is more aggressive than usual. The »International,« the anthem of the socialist workers' movement, is no longer sung; the mayor barely has a chance to speak, and the senior SED district head none at all. »Too late, too late,« chants the crowd. Banners read, »There's a storm brewing« and »The SED has got to go.« The draft travel law and the leadership's inability to implement visible change have apparently brought the situation to a head. »We don't need laws – the Wall has got to go!« cries the crowd.

Tuesday, November 7

The entire East German government resigns, after directing a final appeal to the public that, »in this serious situation, all energies be concentrated on keeping up all functions indispensable to the people, society and the economy.« The ministers will remain in office until a new cabinet is formed. Their last decision is to eliminate military instruction in schools.

Conflicts also break out in the other parties traditionally allied with the SED. After a heated debate, the National Democratic Party (NDPD) elects Günter Hartmann its new Chairman. The Liberal Democrats (LDPD), who helped initiate the reforms and thus can get by without a change in leadership, demand an audit of the economy and fundamental economic reforms by the future cabinet.

Wednesday, November 8

For the first time in its history, the Politburo resigns as a group. However, the Central Committee unanimously reelects Egon Krenz to the position of General Secretary. In a speech, Krenz attempts a reckoning with history, in the course of which – to everyone's surprise – he also criticizes his political mentor Erich Honecker.

In the afternoon, some 15,000 Party members gather in East Berlin to square accounts, sometimes in harsh words, with the old leadership. Politburo members Axen, Hager, Krolikowski, Mielke, Mückenberger, Neumann, Stoph, Sindermann and Tisch step down from the highest SED body. In new elections, three candidates lose out. Hans Modrow, Dresden's popular Party chief, is elected to the Politburo and nominated as candidate for the position of Prime Minister.

At the same time, civil rights activist Bärbel Bohley, founder of New Forum, receives confirmation from the East German Ministry of the Interior that her group has officially been recognized as a political force. This corrects the earlier decision that there was no need for opposition groups in East Germany. All districts are informed of the revised decision in Telex no. 52.

In the evening, author Christa Wolf, in the name of numerous artists and representatives of opposition groups, appears on East German television with a dramatic appeal to all potential emigrants that they rethink their decision and stay in the country: »What can we promise you? Not an easy life, but a useful one. Not rapid prosperity, but the opportunity to participate in great changes. We want to take a stand for democratization, free elections, legal security and freedom of movement. It is apparent that decades of encrustation have been broken through in a few weeks. We stand at the very beginning of fundamental changes in our country. Help us form a truly democratic society that preserves the vision of democratic socialism. It's not a dream if you work with us to prevent it being nipped in the bud. We need you. Trust yourself and those of us who want to stay here.«

The flood of emigrants has left significant gaps in the economy, which the government now tries to close with soldiers and members of the security services. The army provides 600 drivers for supply trucks; trained engine drivers, traffic supervisors and shunters from the military are assigned to civilian transport tasks.

Thursday, November 9

The SED Central Committee continues its plenary session. But only 24 hours after their reelection to the Politburo, district memberships again remove first secretaries Hans-Joachim Böhme in Halle, Werner Walde in Cottbus, and Johannes Chemnitzer in Neubrandenburg. Also, Inge Lange, the longtime women's commissioner of the SED Politburo, resigns her post. General confusion reigns. During an afternoon break, the newly-formed Politburo agrees to adopt new regulations for trips to the West by way of a Council of Ministers' resolution, in order to be able to process the continuing stream of emigrants via Czechoslovakia at East Germany's own border crossing points. The modalities will be announced tomorrow.

In the evening, Politburo member Günter Schabowski announces the results of the Central Committee plenary. Towards the end of the press conference, at exactly 6:53 p.m., an Italian journalist asks about the problematic travel law of November 6. At that, Schabowski announces that new regulations on so-called »permanent emigration« have been adopted today. He then reads a press briefing actually intended for tomorrow, explaining that special conditions will no longer be required for applications to the police for private travel. Asked when this will go into force, Schabowski answers, »As far as I know, this is immediate, without delay.«

Shortly thereafter, the AP and DPA wire services report that East

East Germany unexpectadly opens its borders in the night of November 9. Jubilee on the Bornholmer Brücke between East- and West Berlin. (photo by Andreas Schoelzel)

Germany has opened its borders, and the report is the lead story in evening news broadcasts. Thousands of East Berliners thereupon stream to border crossings to find out if the unbelievable news is true. But everything is closed; the officers have not yet received any instructions to open them. Tumultuous scenes ensue. Thousands push forward, and the situation at the barriers becomes dangerous. No one knows for sure if it's a rumor, a mistake, or a real decision. The border police themselves can provide no information and are completely out of their depth. Half an hour before midnight, some border commanders decide on their own to simply open the gates. The report to the top is, » We're flooding.«

Friday, November 10

Long lines of people wait at border crossings to West Germany. In East Berlin, tens of thousands have made outings to the other side during the night, crossing the Wall that has divided the city for 28 years. The border guards are obliging; given the enormous onslaught and the lack of clear regulations, they simply stop checking documents, and East German citizens can travel back and forth completely unhindered. They are awaited on the other side by jubilant West Berliners. Together they climb the Wall in front of the Brandenburg Gate. Champagne corks pop, and there is singing and dancing.

At the same time, the leadership of the National People's Army is considering closing the borders with military force, and several units are placed on heightened alert. But given the enormous flood of people from East to West and the lack of support by Soviet troops in East Germany, this option has been abandoned by evening.

Meanwhile, politics continues as usual. The Executive Committee of the CDU elects Lothar de Mazière its new Chairman. The 49-year-old lawyer has gained prominence for representing draft resistors and as a leader in the Protestant Church. He restores the bond between the CDU and the Church that has long been clouded.

Newly elected FDGB chief Annelis Kimmel announces that the national board of the unions will resign in a bloc on November 29 in order to permit a new beginning.

The tenth meeting of the SED Central Committee ends after three days of discussion. In a communique, it announces that former Central Committee Secretaries Günter Mittag (economy) and Joachim

Herrmann (media) have been expelled from the Central Committee. The Party Control Commission has been instructed to investigate Mittag's blunders.

Afterwards, at a major rally on Berlin's Lustgarten square that attracts 150,000 participants, the SED membership demands an extraordinary Party conference to elect a new Central Committee and initiate fundamental change.

Saturday, November 11

In the last two days, more than four million visas for travel to West Germany and West Berlin have been issued at border crossings and police stations. *Radio DDR* reports West German trains being utilized at 200% capacity, and West Berlin's radio traffic service acknowledges, with resignation, »Pedestrian traffic is at a standstill on Tauentzien Street.« Experts have lost count of how many people have visited the city, whose normal population is 2 million; it could be 500,000 or a million. In the center of the city, traffic has come to a complete halt; the same is true on some subway lines, which are so crowded that people are forced onto the tracks. Lines form everywhere as East Germans wait in front of banks and offices to collect the 100 DM of »welcome money« provided by West Germany to each East German.

It is announced officially that the First District SED Secretary in Perleberg (Schwerin district) has »taken his life as a result of great psychological pressure caused by the political events on November 7.« This is the third suicide of an SED District Secretary in two weeks.

Sunday, November 12

In the morning, a new border crossing point is opened on East Berlin's Potsdamer Platz, the fifth since Friday morning. During the night, construction crews break through several of the Wall's concrete slabs, smooth the ground and restore the road to Potsdamer Platz, once the heart of Berlin traffic. Mayors Erhard Krack (East) and Walter Momper (West) officially open the crossing. The police stations in both halves of the city are connected with one another for the first time in decades by a special telephone line.

The Berlin section of New Forum distributes flyers on the opening of the Wall that read, »Citizens of East Germany! Your spontaneous, fearless declaration of will throughout the land set a peaceful revolution in motion, brought down the Politburo and broke through the Wall. Don't be distracted from the demand for political reconstruction of society! ...We will remain poor for a long time, but we don't want a society in which profiteers and competitive types skim off the cream. You are the heroes of a political revolution, so don't let yourselves be pacified by travel and debt-increasing injections of consumption. Demand that political reforms be implemented.«

Monday, November 13

With only one dissenting vote, Hans Modrow, 61, is asked by the People's Chamber deputies to form a government. The Dresden SED Party chief has for some time been a focus of people's hopes both at home and abroad. The pro-reform, open-minded and confident Modrow, who has no apparent desire for the external trappings of power, was for a long time purposely kept far from the centers of power in East Berlin. In February 1989, Central Committee Secretary Günter Mittag publicly reprimanded him for »bad Party work« in his district.

In contrast, the 82-year-old former Minister for State Security, Erich Mielke, finds himself in an especially difficult position among the People's Chamber deputies. He listens with visible astonishment to numerous expressions of dissatisfaction following a presentation in which he plays down the state security apparatus. Finally, in confused self-justification, he cries out, »But I love you, I love everyone!«

A new mood has developed at the Monday demonstration in Leipzig: »Germany, united Fatherland« is painted in black, red and gold letters on a white banner, and it isn't long before it is taken up as a chant. Other banners demand, »Let's settle scores with the people responsible for the chaos« and »Down with the SED.«

In Dresden (100,000) Karl-Marx-Stadt (50,000), Wismar (20,000), Neuruppin (12,000), Schwerin (8,000), Cottbus (10,000), Magdeburg (10,000), Bautzen (10,000), Heiligenstadt (9,000), Halle (8,000), Sonneberg (7,000), Apolda (5,000), Pößneck (4,000), Neubrandenburg (3,000), and Zwickau (3,000), demonstrators demand a permanent right to travel, »Western money for mature citizens,« a plebiscite on Article 1 of the Constitution (the SED's monopoly of power), and free elections as soon as possible.

Tuesday, November 14

According to a deputy Secretary in the Ministry of Foreign Trade, Christian Meyer, East Germany is considering joining the European Community. First, however, other forms of cooperation must be found.

West German union leader Franz Steinkühler of the IG Metall union warns against a sellout of East Germany. He sees two possible dangers: East Germany could sell »everything that's not nailed down« to the West to obtain hard currency; or, even worse, agencies might specialize in leasing East German workers to West German firms.

Pastor Friedrich Schorlemmer of Democratic Awakening maintains in an interview that the SED is fundamentally capable of reform, and that its internal reformers exhibit startling intellectual potential. However, he doubts that they can regain public trust after forty years.

In the evening, demonstrations are again held in 30 mainly small and middle-sized towns. Participant figures range from 10,000 in Weimar to 7,500 in Nordhausen and 1,500 in Wittenberg.

Wednesday, November 15

Before the commission investigating the circumstances surrounding government suppression of the demonstrations on October 7 and 8, author Christa Wolf says that the leadership around Erich Honecker had mistaken the protests during East Germany's 40th anniversary celebration for a counterrevolution that had to be quelled »by any means.«

According to Siegfried Wittenbeck, an Undersecretary in the Justice Ministry, the judicial system will in future be independent of the state and Party. He also announces the rehabilitation of people wrongfully convicted of crimes and promises new laws covering courts and judges that will increase judicial independence. He admits that in the past, organs of the Party and state had repeatedly attempted to intervene in pending judicial procedures, and insists that such practices must cease once and for all.

Thursday, November 16

Several East German newspapers begin to publish West German television listings. Only a few weeks ago, anyone copying these listings from Western newspapers and distributing them at work was punished.

The Academy of Sciences announces that its former members Ernst Bloch and Robert Havemann are being rehabilitated and their rights and privileges restored. Havemann, a communist, had been an SED deputy to the People's Chamber, but was expelled from the SED and the university in 1964 because of his anti-Stalinist philosophy lectures. In 1977 he was briefly arrested, and then subjected to limitations on his movements and contacts. In 1979 his house arrest was made more severe, and he was also fined for supposed violations of the customs and currency laws. He died in 1982, at the age of 72, in Grünheide, outside East Berlin, following a difficult illness. Ernst Bloch, a philosopher, was attacked as a revisionist in 1956 and forbidden to make any public appearances. He lost his teaching job in 1957 and emigrated to West Germany in 1961.

The continuing flow of travelers to West Germany leads to a rapid fall in the illegal exchange rate in West Berlin's money-changing offices. Some days, the East German mark falls to 20:1 in relation to the West German mark, leading to speculation in East Germany about a possible monetary reform. The President of the State Bank officially denies these rumors.

Serious problems accompany the increase in inner-German contacts. It has become almost impossible to call the other side by telephone. Post Office Director Willi Gülzow announces that the lines to West Berlin and West Germany are completely clogged. He says that demand has skyrocketed in recent days, and calls this the price for neglecting the situation for decades.

This evening, demonstrations take place in 20 cities. In Rostock, 15,000 people march to the district headquarters of the Stasi to demand its elimination; in both Erfurt and Gera, 10,000 demand an end to the SED's monopoly on power.

Friday, November 17

The new East German government is presented in East Berlin. Instead of 44 ministries, there are now only 28. The ministries that centrally directed each individual branch of the economy have been eliminated. Seventeen ministers still belong to the SED, four to the LDPD, three to the CDU, and two each to the NDPD and the Peasants' Party. Nine served in the old government. The Ministry for State Security, which has become a focus of public criticism, is dissolved and replaced by a smaller Office of National Security.

In the subsequent debate, Modrow advocates a treaty federation with West Germany (»cooperative coexistence«) and stability in foreign trade, which he calls a »question of survival.« East Germany, he says, is not currently capable of drafting an economic program or a state budget for the coming year. The new government must first realistically calculate its revenues and expenses.

The well-known dissident Rudolf Bahro, who was imprisoned in 1977 and then expelled to the West in 1979, where he made a name for himself in the Green Party, announces his return to East Germany. At the same time, in an interview he voices his concern about current developments. »The most important thing on German soil today is that the part that brought a democratic, political revolution into being should not immediately be sucked up by the economically terribly superior, but at the same time suicidal, western system. The crucial thing right now is to maintain the autonomy of the political processes in East Germany. It would be absurd, just at the moment when East Germany is really owned by the people, to have to assess its sellout in three or four years.«

The Ministry of the Interior provides an interim report on the emerging variety of organizations in the country. It announces the existence of 154 political associations in East Germany and says 37 more have applied for recognition.

Saturday, November 18

On this second weekend of open borders, millions of East Germans are on the road, visiting nearby West German cities or West Berlin. East German trains are at »four hundred percent capacity,« and there are tumultuous scenes on the platforms. Despite rapid processing of documents at highway border crossings, the lines stretch for kilometers. The attraction is not only the West's newness, but also the West German government's »welcome money,« which – aside from the permitted currency exchange of 15 DM per person per year in East Germany – is the only legal way to obtain Western currency. But for many it's not enough, as the full store windows are too much of a draw. Once again, large amounts of East German currency flow into exchange offices, even though the exchange rate of 1:12 to 1:20 continues to be unfavorable. Because of this situation, Prime Minister Modrow warns his countrymen and women not to »throw away« their hard-earned money in the West.

Council of State Chairman Egon Krenz swears in the new coalition government. Instead of an oath, this consists of a simple handshake. But the problem remains that this is not a democratic government that was the product of free elections. Nor are the new political forces represented; the government is merely transitional.

New Forum's first officially sanctioned rally takes place on Dimitroff Square in Leipzig, but because of the exodus of travelers to the West, attendance is lower than expected. Some 20,000 people gather to demand free elections and freedom of the press.

In Plauen, too, 10,000 march to the town hall, and in Suhl, in Thuringia, roughly 5,000 respond to a call from New Forum; 7,000 do the same in Eberswalde-Finow. Repeated demands include radical economic reform, democratization of political life and environmental protection. In Dresden, 50,000 rally for protection of the city's landmark buildings and an end to the selling off of national art and cultural treasures.

Sunday, November 19

Thousands of Berliners demonstrate for free elections, a new constitution, and fundamental democratic reforms. They condemn the renaming of the Ministry for State Security as the Office of National Security, calling it a ruse, and demand the exposure of all Stasi informers in workplaces. Various artists' groups have called this unsanctioned rally, which is characterized by unusually original banners and posters. After the demonstration, these are deposited in front of the People's Chamber and ultimately become part of the collection of Berlin's Museum of German History.

Monday, November 20

Figures are released today showing that nearly 100,000 East Germans have emigrated to West Germany since the beginning of November.

According to a spot survey of 2,180 East Germans at six border crossings by the FORSA opinion research institute of Dortmund, the citizens' group New Forum would be the strongest group in parliament if elections were held today. It would receive 22% of all votes, the LDPD 15%, the SED only 14%, the CDU 12%, and the SDP 10%. The Peasants' Party (DBD) would receive only 3%, and the NDPD 2%.

More and more, public debate revolves around future economic policy and foreign trade relationships. This is a result of the seven prerequisites named by Bonn if West Germany is to become economically involved: 1. free elections; 2. recognition of opposition parties; 3. abandonment of the SED monopoly of power; 4. introduction of market economy mechanisms; 5. creation of a hard-currency fund for East German travelers; 6. elimination of the required minimum exchange for Western travelers to the East; 7. easing of travel restrictions on West German citizens in the East.

Prime Minister Modrow issues a memorandum in which the new government advocates closer cooperation with the European Community. It also for the first time proposes political cooperation. According to the memo, East Germany is prepared to promote the overall process of European integration within the context of its own interests. The country wishes to develop its relationship with the EC »rapidly, cooperatively, and constructively.«

Hundreds of thousands again demonstrate this evening. In Leipzig alone, roughly a quarter of a million participants are counted in the traditional Monday demonstration. They chant »Germany, united fatherland,« and banners demand a plebiscite on reunification. Attacks on the SED leadership become harsher. Speakers claim that the Central Committee has purchased an island in the Caribbean and that Margot Honecker regularly flies to Paris to shop. They demand that the Party leadership be hauled before a people's tribunal.

In Halle, 50,000 people demonstrate for free elections and the »irreversible renewal of social processes.« Speaking to 50,000 demonstrators in Karl-Marx-Stadt, a representative of New Forum proposes forming a human chain across the entire country to demand democratic renewal. »Next Sunday at 12 o'clock, let's form a human chain from Fichtelberg to Cape Arkona, from Wartburg to the Neisse. With this human chain, on the ›Sunday of the Dead‹, we will bury the past so we can get to work on a new future.«

Today's demonstrations, which take place in 20 towns, are directed increasingly at the district and county headquarters of the State Security. Protesters demand access to the files and dissolution of the secret service. Candles are lit at the entrances.

Tuesday, November 21

The opposition group Democracy Now invites all democratic parties and movements in East Germany to a »round table« in order to agree upon joint action. The LDPD is the first party to accept the invitation.

Horst Kaminsky, president of the State Bank, asks that banks, like factories, be granted economic independence. According to his figures, the country's credit institutes presently have reserves of 250 billion marks and 150 billion in financing credits. There are 570 billion in building, machine and investment assets, as opposed to 60 billion marks in investment credits. The monetary and credit volumes are met completely by economic output, Kaminsky assures an interviewer from the *National-Zeitung* newspaper.

Wednesday, November 22

The SED voices its support for a Round Table. The Politburo agrees to a suggestion that it take up contacts at the highest levels with the parties of the »democratic bloc« and other political groups in the country. The spokesman for the group Democratic Awakening, Pastor Rainer Eppelmann, welcomes the SED's willingness as a »good sign.« Jutta Seidel of New Forum also agrees.

In East Berlin, charges of inflicting serious bodily harm are brought against a policeman accused of pushing an arrested demonstrator down a flight of steps at a police station. A total of 76 investigations are under way of members of the security forces, 43 of them involving unknown suspects. Most involve charges such as intentional injury, coercion and defamation.

Debates continue about the large-scale purchase of subsidized goods by foreigners, mainly from neighboring Poland. Indignation has grown among East Germans as many products become scarce, especially since the establishment of a so-called »Polish market« in West Berlin where more and more East German products are being sold.

Thursday, November 23

The Council of Ministers adopts measures to prevent smuggling and speculation. Beginning immediately, certain goods may be sold only to East Germans and to foreigners who live and work in the country. Shoppers may be asked to present personal identification in order to purchase heavily subsidized products. East Berlin had already instituted this practice once, in the late 1950s. Back then, the government was trying to limit the effect of open borders on trade; because of the favorable exchange rate and relatively low prices in the eastern part of the city, West Berliners were attempting to take advantage of the currency gap by buying East German products on a large scale, further reducing the supply of goods. West Berliners also took full advantage of the favorable exchange rate for services.

Similar problems are arising now; since the opening of the borders on November 9, nearly three billion East German marks have been brought into West Berlin and West Germany illegally, according to official figures. For this reason, the citizens' group New Forum appeals to its countrymen not to use the open borders for speculation and black-marketeering. »Don't participate in the sellout of our country,« they urge. »Don't take black market jobs, don't sell art treasures and subsidized goods, don't exchange East German marks at fraudulent rates; those same East German marks will later buy us out of house and home.«

The East German CDU also makes clear demands. It calls for free elections by mid-1990 at the latest, along with a new election law that will make it possible to choose freely among people, parties and programs and ensure equal conditions during the campaign. It asks further that a new constitution be adopted by plebiscite, one which does not ensure the SED a monopoly of power.

The head of the newly-created Office of National Security, Lieutenant General Wolfgang Schwanitz, announces that 8,000 secret service personnel will be cut.

In the evening, the film *Spur der Steine* (Track of the Stones), banned by the SED more than 20 years ago, is shown in East Berlin's International Movie Theater. At a press conference following the screening, director Frank Beyer says, »When I ask myself why these conditions were maintained until only a few weeks ago, I come up with three reasons: 1. The Soviet tanks in the country. It's true that these tanks haven't been available as a repressive potential for several years – that is, since glasnost and perestroika were established in the Soviet Union – but probably some time had to pass before people understood the new opportunities to achieve democracy. 2. Because it was antifascists who introduced the Stalinist variety of socialism here. To fight Stalinism we would have had to fight antifascists, and many did not want to. There is a great deal of respect in this country for those who were forced to spend many years of their life in exile or in prisons or camps. This respect should be maintained despite the necessary discussions on deep-seated changes in the country. 3. Even the slightest attempt at rebellion was immediately suppressed by those in power. The potential for protest, even the mere suggestion of it, was dissipated; those who rebelled were isolated, forced out of the country, and had their citizenship revoked.«

Friday, November 24

In a poll to determine East Germans' favorite politician, Egon Krenz receives only 9.6%, not exactly a flattering figure for a head of state. Premier Hans Modrow is much more popular, receiving 42% of the votes. His calm pragmatism, free of rhetoric or false promises, clearly encourages trust and sympathy. (However, 33% say they don't like any politician at the moment.)

The incidents in East Berlin on October 7 and 8 are the subject of a public trial of policeman Horst L., charged by the prosecution with inflicting serious bodily harm. Many of his colleagues are present in the courtroom when the defendant withdraws his confession. He denies pushing the victim down the stairs or shoving him. Asked about this change of heart, he says, »During the interrogation I was under extreme psychological pressure.« He adds that, in conversation with others, he had concluded that »it doesn't matter anyway.« His colleagues call out, »Just admit that they betrayed us.« The court sentences Horst L. to one year and two months' imprisonment without parole, plus payment of compensation.

In the afternoon, another wave of travel to the West begins. The East

German railway makes extra trains available. Lines continue to form outside branches of the State Bank to exchange the permitted 15 DM at a rate of 1:1. State Bank President Kaminsky announces that 12.8 million East Germans have obtained 200 million DM from the bank in this way since the borders were opened. The money – mainly in small bills – has been brought in from the West Berlin regional bank by truck.

According to 83% of the respondents to a survey by East Berlin sociologists, East Germany should remain a sovereign, socialist country. Only 10% support unification with West Germany.

Saturday, November 25

Egon Krenz visits Leipzig and voices his »deep concern« at the city's decay, »because this once again makes plain the extent to which Leipzig was neglected by the central government in past years.« The head of state and Party chief says that »it has never been as clear to me as it is today what signals were sent from Leipzig regarding our country, the renewal of socialism, and this difficult stage that lies before us.«

In an interview, Rainer Eppelmann, the spokesman for Democratic Awakening, says the opposition should cooperate with a »transformed SED.« He maintains that no political force can lead East Germany out of its crisis by itself, and confirms that former SED members have joined Democratic Awakening. Eppelmann believes all parties, including the SED, are capable of fundamental change.

In the evening, 5,000 residents of the city of Plauen demonstrate in snow and ice. Banners overwhelmingly support the »reunification« of the two German states.

Sunday, November 26

Famous personalities and representatives of grass-roots groups issue a statement entitled »For our Country,« in which they maintain, »Our country is in a deep crisis. We neither can, nor do we wish, to live as we used to. Non-violently, through mass demonstrations, the people have forced a process of revolutionary renewal that is being completed with breathtaking speed. We have only a little time left to influence the various possibilities offered as ways out of the crisis. Either we insist on East Germany's independence and attempt, with all our strength and in cooperation with those states and interest groups that are prepared to do so, to develop in our country a society of solidarity in which peace and social justice, freedom for the individual, freedom of movement for all and environmental protection are guaranteed. Or we must accept the possibility that, through heavy economic pressures and unacceptable conditions imposed by influential West German economic and political circles in exchange for helping East Germany, a sellout of our material and moral values will begin and, sooner or later, the German Democratic Republic will be coopted by the Federal Republic. Let us take the first path.« The signers include the authors Volker Braun, Stefan Heym, and Christa Wolf, the church's General Superintendent Günter Krusche, and Pastor Friedrich Schorlemmer.

It becomes known that the government and the opposition will meet at a Round Table for the first time on December 7 to consider joint steps on the road to democratization. All controversial issues are to be negotiated.

Monday, November 27

Responding to years of demands, mainly from the church, a pilot project on civil alternatives to military service begins in Dresden. For the first time in East Germany, 25 young men will perform voluntary service in the Friedrichstadt district hospital. Among them are men who refuse to serve under arms*, as well as total conscientious objectors.

At the Office of National Security, long-heralded talks take place with the Presidium of the Association of Jewish Communities on right-wing, neo-Nazi and anti-Semitic tendencies in East Germany. The guests criticize the fact that insufficient notice has been taken of the incidents registered in various districts. They point to the appearance of flyers by the right-wing »Republikaner« that purposely exploit existing xenophobic tendencies.

At this evening's Monday demonstrations in several cities, the issue of German unity plays a central role. In Leipzig, 200,000 people now

* *These conscripts, known as Bausoldaten, refuse to carry weapons and instead perform tasks such as trench-digging.*

demand not only free elections, freedom of opinion and punishment of former SED leaders, but also, in ringing chants, »Germany, united fatherland.«

Tuesday, November 28

Chancellor Helmut Kohl announces a so-called ten-point plan to overcome German division. He proposes gradually expanding relations between West and East Germany until they become a single federated state. However, Bonn links economic aid to »practical prerequisites.« These include free elections, an end to the SED's monopoly of power, release of political prisoners and dismantling of the planned economy in favor of »free market conditions.« The goal is development of a confederative structure; that is, the creation of a »federated state system in Germany.« There is no direct reference to an immediate unification of the two German states. Egon Krenz responds by insisting on the existence of two independent, sovereign German states.

The Christian Democratic regional newspaper *Der Demokrat* reports from Rostock that, until recently, personnel from the Ministry for State Security at the city's main post office had been reading all incoming mail from West Germany and the West in general. An entire floor of the post office had been set aside for them. Internally, this department was nicknamed »Herbert.«

Wednesday, November 29

According to the general superintendent of the Protestant Church of Berlin-Brandenburg, Günter Krusche, East Germany must follow a path independent of West Germany. Says Krusche, »We should not give up the point of view of justice in favor of the point of view of the free market.«

Harry Tisch, Chairman of the Trade Union Federation until a few weeks ago, is expelled from the FDGB. Its entire national board resigns, and a working secretariat will carry out its functions for the present.

Culture Minister Dietmar Keller announces that pre-censorship of books will cease on December 1, and new private publishing companies will be permitted to form. There have only been 78 state-licensed publishers up to now, and each manuscript required written permission from the Culture Ministry before publication, even Shakespeare's dramas and Goethe's »Faust.«

This evening, tens of thousands again demonstrate for guarantees of the democratic gains made so far and against SED hegemony. Even in a relatively small town like Limbach-Oberfrohna, in Saxony, 5,000 people take part in a rally; in Ilmenau, in Thuringia, the figure is 6,000, in Halberstadt more than 5,000. In Leipzig, thousands of SED members gather on Dimitroffplatz, demanding from their leaders a consistent dismantling of privileges and total disclosure of corruption and abuse of power. But there is no support for the demand that the Party dissolve and reform itself. Kohl's 10-point plan is rejected and East German independence advocated.

Thursday, November 30

Minister of the Economy Christa Luft announces for the first time that East Germany currently owes ten billion dollars in net payments. However, she also assures the public that individual savings are secure.

The well-known scientist Manfred von Ardenne warns in an interview with *Neues Deutschland* against halfway measures; he says radical structural changes are necessary in the economy and society. In his opinion, enterprises must be given greater independence, the state's monopoly on foreign trade eliminated, and the transition to a market economy initiated. State revenues should be obtained through taxes, not by skimming off enterprise profits.

The public prosecutor's office begins investigations of six top members of the old leadership, including Erich Honecker, on charges of abuse of power and wasteful misuse of public property. The investigation concentrates on several state-run hunting preserves and luxurious summer homes.

In the evening, over 10,000 residents of Erfurt demonstrate in a show of indignation at the privileges enjoyed by SED leaders, including former SED district head Gerhard Müller. They demand an immediate report on their abuse of office. A number of other cities have already held warning strikes for the same reason. In Rostock (15,000) and Gera (6,000), marchers demand the elimination of the Stasi.

December 1989

Friday, December 1

By an overwhelming majority, the People's Chamber decides to eliminate the SED's constitutionally-anchored monopoly of power. This means elimination of the first clause of Article 1, which states that East German socialism is led by »the working class and its Marxist-Leninist party.« The CDU loses its bid to also eliminate Article 1's statement that East Germany is a socialist country.

The chairman of the parliamentary committee investigating corruption and abuse of power, Heinrich Toeplitz (CDU), discusses the behavior of the police and security forces, asking who had trained them to mistreat and torment suspects in custody. He insists it cannot be coincidental that police units in places as far apart as Dresden, Bautzen and Berlin had harassed arrested suspects »using the same methods.« Such methods, he said, should have ceased with the end of the Nazi period.

The head of the newly-created Office of National Security, General Wolfgang Schwanitz, informs the visibly affected deputies that he can say little about these actions, since he has inherited only two empty safes from his predecessor, State Security Minister Erich Mielke.

Singer-songwriter Wolf Biermann, whose East German citizenship was revoked in 1976, is allowed to appear in East Germany again for the first time. He sings for an audience of 6,000 in Leipzig. »The Federal Republic is not the solution to the problems of humanity that we all face,« he says, referring to the demand for reunification that has been heard of late in Leipzig. »I am not happy about this ›Germany, Germany über alles‹ mood. We would be pretty silly – you would be pretty silly – to go backwards to the old Reich à la Kohl. Thank you very much!« he calls to the audience, which applauds his words.

For the first time in East Germany, a smog alarm is issued in Leipzig today. The air is so thick in this city, surrounded by chemical factories, that it calls for a level-two alarm and cancellation of an evening soccer game between teams from Leipzig and Dresden.

Saturday, December 2

Media response to a call for a general strike by New Forum representatives in Karl-Marx-Stadt is strongly negative, as it would only further damage the already-weak economy. In response to these criticisms, the initiators limit their intentions, saying that if demands for democratization – such as setting a date for free elections – are met by December 6, the strike should not be held.

The newly-founded Green Party acknowledges a dangerous increase in anti-Semitism and right-wing tendencies in East Germany. It sees a direct connection with the increase in right-wing radicalism in Western European countries, but also points to fertile soil in East Germany itself. The »Republikaner« have formed their first underground groups.

Residents of Rostock county reveal a storage depot in Kavelstorf to be a transfer point for international weapons sales by the state-owned IMES corporation. The business apparently has contacts in Africa, Latin America and the Middle East. The hard currency earned through weapons dealing was transferred to the »Commercial Coordination« section run by Undersecretary Alexander Schalck-Golodkowski, according to Director General Ehrhardt Wichert. Handguns, ammunition and trucks are found in the main hall, which is immediately sealed.

In the evening, thousands of SED party members gather in front of the Central Committee building in Berlin demanding radical renewal of the Party, an extraordinary party congress, total exposure of Party privileges and the resignation of the entire Politburo.

At demonstrations in over 20 other cities, including Plauen (14,000), Magdeburg (10,000), Görlitz, Annaberg and Finsterwalde (5,000 each), Potsdam, Weißwasser (3,000 each), and Rostock (2,000), the demands that the SED give up power and the secret police be eliminated become louder.

Sunday, December 3

In the afternoon, hundreds of thousands of people form a human chain across the country, from north to south and from east to west, as a sign of hope and the determination to achieve democratic renewal. At exactly 12 noon, they link hands and step onto the roadways; in larger towns, traffic comes to a halt for 15 minutes, with many drivers leaving their cars to join the chain. Lit candles once again symbolize non-violence.

Alexander Schalk-Golodkowski, Undersecretary and procurer of hard-currency, has fled. Government spokesman Meyer announces that the chief of the »Commercial Coordination« section has been stripped of his offices. Schalk only yesterday took part in official negotiations in Bonn. His present location is unknown.

Former General Secretary Erich Honecker, ex-Premier Willi Stoph, ex-union leader Harry Tisch, ex-Parliamentary President Horst Sindermann, and ex-Minister of State Security Erich Mielke, as well as other senior functionaries, are expelled from the SED for serious violations of its statute. Harry Tisch, ex-Economics Secretary Günter Mittag, and district chiefs Müller (Erfurt) and Albrecht (Suhl) are arrested.

This afternoon, responding to the overwhelming demand of the day before and to pressure from the newly-elected district secretaries, the SED Central Committee and Politburo resign. In place of the Central Committee, a working committee assumes the duties of Party leadership. At its first meeting, it agrees to appoint an inner-party investigative commission under the chairmanship of Gregor Gysi, who has the main Central Committee offices sealed off, bank accounts frozen, and the central database secured.

Revolts take place in a number of prisons. In East Berlin, inmates demand a general amnesty, better conditions, codetermination and higher pay for their work.

An Independent Women's Organization is formed at a meeting in East Berlin's Volksbühne theater. In its manifesto, it calls for clear reform of the political and economic systems. However, it opposes reunification, saying that this would represent »three steps backward« for women. Several »immediate demands« are directed at the government, including creation of a Council of Ministers' fund for the promotion of women, radio and television broadcast slots, and establishment of women's committees at all parliamentary levels.

In the evening, demonstrators in numerous cities march to the county headquarters of the Office of National Security and demand public supervision of its activities or its dissolution.

Monday, December 4

An appeal to all members of the »Commercial Coordination« section is read out over the radio: »Call staff meetings to install supervisory groups to prevent further illegal dealings. Inform the German People's Police and the public. Cooperate with other enterprises and with citizens' groups that you trust. If necessary, decide upon joint supervisory measures and be sure to make them public.«

The National People's Army also begins to take security measures, canceling low-flight exercises in the neighborhood of the Kavelstorf weapons depot. The public in the area is extremely worried by the discovery of huge stores of ammunition in simple lightweight structures, and demands that they be removed to more secure depots.

The SED Central Committee is obviously attempting to destroy or ship out incriminating documents. The head of the finance section is arrested. Staff at the Berlin-Schönefeld airport point out that two special planes are being loaded with files, preparatory to being flown to Romania.

The CDU and the LDPD announce that they are leaving the so-called democratic bloc. They maintain that cooperation with other political and social forces in the country is possible only at the Round Table. The CDU Presidium also demands the resignation of Egon Krenz as head of the Council of State and Chairman of the National Defense Council.

The various discoveries also lead to other consequences, as cases of vigilante justice increase. Prominent figures in politics, culture and the economy issue an appeal for a security partnership between citizens' committees and organs of the state: »Throughout the country there have been manifestations of fury and indignation over abuse of power, corruption, crime and attempts to mask criminal actions. We share this fury and concern. There are signs that actions are emerging from this justified fury that could end by endangering people's safety and life.« This, they say, must not be permitted.

For the first time, members of the People's Police and the security forces take to the streets to protest abuse of office, corruption and the destruction of files. They say they will do everything they can to expose these crimes.

The head of the Office of National Security, General Wolfgang Schwanitz, announces that 10,000 former employees of the Ministry for State Security have been laid off.

In the evening, as every Monday, over a quarter of a million people demonstrate in numerous East German cities. In Leipzig, where 150,000 people gather, many black, red and gold flags are in evidence. On homemade posters, Erich Honecker is portrayed in a prison uniform, and banners read »SED – kiss our asses!,« »Corrupt SED nobility to the stocks!,« and »Stasi to the factories.« Because many of the demonstrators are directing their anger at the district headquarters of the Stasi, located nearby, representatives of the citizens' groups and lawyer Wolfgang Schnur of Democratic Awakening are permitted to enter the Stasi stronghold in order to head off a storm. With the help of the police, a spontaneously-formed citizens' committee seals many rooms to prevent further destruction of files.

Tuesday, December 5

Prosecutor General Günter Wendland steps down. His successor, Harri Harland, announces that former SED General Secretary Erich Honecker and other dismissed representatives of the old party leadership are under house arrest in the gated community of Wandlitz, north of Berlin. He says this measure represents a sort of »national emergency.«

In Berlin, a man is arrested at the back entrance of the »House of the Electroindustry« with two suitcases full of money – a half million West German marks and several hundred thousand East German marks – and documents. The man, who claims to be an institute director, turns out to belong to the Office of National Security.

In Suhl, 2,000 people force their way into the district Office of National Security after tear gas is fired to keep them back. The head of the office later admits that in Suhl, as in Leipzig, Erfurt and Berlin, documents have been destroyed on a large scale. In Erfurt and Dresden, citizens also force their way into district administrative offices to stop the destruction of additional incriminating material.

The arms, technology and special equipment of workers' militias will be confiscated immediately, according to a Ministry of the Interior spokesperson. »Tanks, grenade launchers, recoilless firearms and flak will be taken from factories to Ministry locations.« Weapons stores in factories will be removed by the police.

The situation is worsening in correctional institutions. Inmates of Bautzen prison are staging a hunger strike for review of their convictions and higher pay. The director of prisons, General Lustig, announces that East German prisoners annually produce 12.5 billion marks' worth of industrial goods, and acknowledges the inmates' »excellent discipline.«

Wednesday, December 6

Bowing to continuing protests, Egon Krenz resigns as head of the Council of State and Chairman of the National Defense Council. His deputy as head of the Council of State, Professor Manfred Gerlach (LDPD), takes over.

The search for fugitive ex-Undersecretary Schalck-Golodkowski continues. Israel denies his presence in the country, police are looking in West Germany, and a request has also been lodged with Switzerland.

A spokesperson for the Ministry of the Interior announces that, as part of the dismantling of the system of privileges for Party leaders, special »free passage« IDs for Party and state functionaries will be canceled immediately. These had permitted the intentional flouting of traffic laws, such as the maximum speed limit.

It becomes known that the man who attempted to remove two suitcases full of money from the Berlin »House of the Electroindustry« has hanged himself while in investigative custody. His identity as a colonel with the Office of National Security had already been established.

In a special broadcast by the youth program *Elf 99*, former SED Central Committee Secretary Herbert Häber, who had also belonged to the Politburo for a year, relates how, after substantive disagreements with General Secretary Honecker, he had been removed from his posts and committed to a psychiatric clinic as a hopeless case.

In the late evening, fugitive Alexander Schalck-Golodkowski surrenders to the West Berlin authorities and is jailed in Moabit Prison.

Thursday, December 7

The central Round Table meets for the first time in the Dietrich Bonhoeffer building in Berlin. Fourteen parties, political groups and organizations take part, all with different expectations.

Following a heated debate, they agree to the following statement of function: »The participants in the Round Table are meeting out of deep concern about our country, which finds itself in crisis, and its independence and long-term development. They require the release of information on the ecological, economic and financial situation in our country. Although the Round Table cannot exercise parliamentary or government functions, it will offer the public proposals on how to overcome the crisis. It demands that it be informed promptly by the People's Chamber and the executive of important legal, economic and financial decisions, and that it be included. It sees itself as an element of public oversight in our country. It plans to continue its work until free, democratic and secret elections are held.« After the first day of discussion, the participants have already agreed on a concrete result: The first free parliamentary elections in East Germany will be held on May 6, 1990.

It seems urgent that the various political groupings reach some accommodation, for the situation in the country is worsening. As government spokesman Meyer announces, increasing dissatisfaction with attempts to suppress evidence of wrongdoing, and the slow pace of investigations to expose abuse of office and corruption, have been leading to spontaneous action that »hinders the work of government organs and is thus not in the citizens' best interest.« Wolfgang Schwanitz, head of the Office of National Security, is forced to admit that four district offices have had to cease operations, while the work of others has been greatly restricted. In Berlin, as a result of heavy public pressure, the headquarters of the former Ministry of State Security on Normannenstrasse must be opened up briefly for viewing by a supervisory group to prevent destruction of files. However, »there is not yet any talk of« declaring a state of emergency.

A spokesperson for the Prosecutor General's office announces the release of 15,000 people in a partial amnesty. Those not falling under the amnesty include people suspected of corruption, abuse of office, and enrichment, or those against whom investigations have been initiated in this connection.

The public is appalled by the news that the Berlin cemetery of the »Adass Yisroel« Jewish community has been desecrated again.

Demonstrations are held today in Berlin, as they are on the seventh of every month; on Alexanderplatz, there is the usual whistling for the elections of May 7. This time, the roughly 2,000 protesters march through the city center and then aim a chorus of whistles at the City Council building, announcing their demand for free and unrigged elections. At the Central Committee building, they call for a revision of the results of the spring elections. They chant, »We don't need Krenz or Kohl – only governing ourselves will make us feel whole!« Demonstrations also take place in 20 other towns. The largest are in Erfurt and Rostock, with 15,000 participants each, and they loudly support the Round Table's demand for complete elimination of the Stasi.

Friday, December 8

The People's Chamber begins to draft a new election law. All Round Table participant organizations not represented in parliament are asked to cooperate.

Defense Minister Theodor Hoffmann tells parliamentary President Maleuda that the army is concerned at the »decrease in order« in East Germany: »We fear for the security of this Republic, over which we stand guard.« He is especially worried that weapons and ammunition from army depots could fall into the wrong hands.

Finance Minister Uta Nickel presents the first economic stocktaking, which reveals a budget deficit of 17 billion marks.

Trade Minister Manfred Flegel points to the complicated situation in the supply of industrial goods. Since the domestic debt was revealed to be 135 billion marks, the public has rushed to buy up quality consumer items such as washing machines, refrigerators, color televisions, furs and jewelry. The supply shortages thus caused cannot be corrected in the short term. However, supply for the coming holidays is largely ensured, and there is no reason to worry about the East German currency.

Former SED Politburo members Erich Mielke, Willi Stoph, Günter Kleiber and Werner Krolikowski are arrested. For the present, exceptions are made for Erich Honecker, because of his poor health, and Hermann Axen, who is in Moscow for an eye operation. The Prosecutor's office announces that they have been charged with corruption, abuse of office, and seriously damaging the economy.

In the evening, the first part of the early SED Party Conference demanded by the membership begins in Berlin. The conference is expected to elect new leaders. In the future, instead of a General Secretary, the SED will be headed by a Chairman directly elected by the party conference. Dresden Mayor Wolfgang Berghofer, who heads up the gathering and enjoys the support of many delegates, declares that he will not be running for the office of Chairman.

Saturday, December 9

After 16 hours, the SED has a new Chairman. Gregor Gysi, a 41-year-old lawyer who once defended dissidents, has been elected by an overwhelming majority of 95.3% of the delegates. Instead of flowers, he is given a huge broom – to ensure a thorough housecleaning.

Illegal financial transactions by the union leadership, including the wrongful diversion of donations to Third World solidarity funds to organize domestic political rallies, lead to the resignation of the FDGB Secretariat and its new Chairperson, Annelis Kimmel. She has been in office only five weeks and was unable to gain the confidence of the union membership.

Sunday, December 10

District offices of the former Ministry for State Security in Neubrandenburg and Suhl become the first to close up shop. Although there is no formal agreement as yet on the opposition demand to eliminate the Office of National Security, officials in places where pressure is greatest have already drawn their own conclusions. Citizens' committees and independent investigative commissions now secure the files, take complaints and bring charges.

A new political group, the »Carnations,« is formed. It aims to found a Marxist party and, in its first declaration, supports a socialist path of development for East Germany.

Participants in the demonstrations that take place this weekend throughout the country insist upon the irreversible nature of the changes so far and on continued reform. Rostock demonstrators also warn against the resurgence of fascist forces. Large groups voice opposition to the »co-optation« of East Germany by West Germany. In Cottbus, demonstrators demand the establishment of the rule of law and punishment of abuse of office and corruption. Children and young people demonstrate in Leipzig and Magdeburg for schools »that are fun.« Strikes by many students have already led to the introduction of a five-day school week. In Plauen, 15,000 people take to the streets; the dominant subject is German unification. In Erfurt, hundreds of people form a »citizens' bulwark« against the threatened decay of architecturally valuable buildings and plans to demolish the historic city center, East Germany's largest extended landmark.

Monday, December 11

Developments in East Germany are the subject of the first four-power conference in 18 years. The ambassadors of the United States, France, Great Britain and the Soviet Union meet in the Allied Control Commission building in West Berlin to discuss possible consequences of the changes in East Germany and the future inclusion of West Berlin in the process of European integration.

The Ministry of the Interior confiscates the weapons of leading functionaries to prevent any accidental overreactions in the present tense situation.

In Karl-Marx-Stadt, 40,000 people demonstrate for reunification. Chancellor Helmut Kohl's 10-point plan, which provides for the gradual formation of a confederation, is especially popular. Vociferous disagreements break out at the traditional Monday demonstration in Leipzig between supporters and opponents of German unification. While some unfurl banners reading »Thank God the West is coming« and chant »Germany, united fatherland,« others carry placards announcing, »We won't sell ourselves out« and shout »GDR, GDR.«

The demonstrations have visibly changed in composition. In October and early November, the predominant tone was set by members of the alternative milieu, students and intellectuals, people who now make up the leadership of the new opposition parties or can be found in independent working groups and at the Round Table. Workers now set the mood on the streets, bringing other interests to bear.

Tuesday, December 12

Premier Hans Modrow meets in Potsdam with U.S. Secretary of State James Baker, who voices his support for the process of democratic reform in East Germany. Modrow advocates progressing from dialogue to cooperation. The subject of German unification is not discussed. A few days ago, Russian President Mikhail Gorbachev and US President George Bush agreed that this is not yet on the agenda.

The first prison inmates are released under an amnesty adopted by the Council of State. The amnesty, the third since 1987, includes everyone »sentenced to up to three years for intentional or negligent wrongdoing« before December 6 of this year, regardless of whether the judgment has become final or not. Exceptions are serious crimes such as robbery, extortion, intentional homicide, hooliganism and sex crimes.

Throughout East Germany, Ministry for State Security mail-surveillance offices in post offices are shut down. At a local press conference in Magdeburg, secret service agents reveal that these special post office departments not only opened mail, but also tapped and recorded telephone conversations.

Wednesday, December 13

The right-wing »Republikaner« party hopes to take part in East German parliamentary elections together with its »sister party« of the same name, according to its West Berlin Chairman Carsten Pagel. He says his party has been encouraged to campaign by the demands for reunification in East Germany.

Günter Hartmann, Chairman of the National Democratic Party (NDPD), says today that he opposes German reunification but advocates a confederation of the two states. He claims reunification would be »absolutely outmoded, against the interests of our people, and thus not politically feasible.« It would mean nothing less than cooptation of East Germany by the Federal Republic. »Such reunification would soon bring us full shops, but also a rapid dismantling of social programs; we would certainly soon have more modern equipment in the factories, but just as surely, hundreds of thousands of unemployed.«

As a worthy conclusion to this autumn's demonstration movement, church representatives and democratic groups propose a silent commemoration of the victims of Stalinism in East Germany, without posters or chants.

Thursday, December 14

The government accedes to demands by opposition groups at the Round Table and agrees to the gradual elimination of the Office of National Security, which succeeded the Ministry for State Security. A supervisory commission will oversee its dismantling.

The citizens' group Democracy Now responds to the changing mood in the country with a »Three-Stage Plan for National Unification.« This is an attempt to replace the appeal on the street for immediate unification with a long-term strategy, under which the process of democratic consolidation in East Germany will be coupled with a gradual political rapprochement between the two German states, so that, in the end, »a new German political unity, based in a society in solidarity,« will emerge. The first phase would require political reforms in both Germanies: electoral, constitutional, and economic reform in East Germany, social and ecological reform in West Germany. Then the basic treaty would be changed to a national treaty, creating a federation with dual citizenship and dual membership in the European Community and Comecon. Finally, in the third phase, following withdrawal of Allied troops and adoption of a European Peace Treaty, a »Federation of German States« will produce political unity.

According to the Berlin Conference of Bishops, there are currently 6.2 million Christians in East Germany, or 37.4% of the population. Five point one million belong to the Federation of Protestant Churches, 1.05 million claim the Catholic faith, and 71,450 belong to other churches or religious denominations.

Elmar Faber, chief of the publishing committee of the Leipzig Association of Publishers and Booksellers, provides information on changes in the East German publishing landscape. Several new private firms have appeared, such as the nonfiction publishers LinksDruck and BasisDruck, and existing state publishers have opened themselves up to new forms of cooperation, such as joint ventures with West German publishing houses.

In the evening, over 10,000 residents of Erfurt demonstrate for democracy and a mature East Germany. Representatives of New Forum advocate the preservation of social values which they say must be maintained in the process of unifying the two German states. In Halle and Gera, rallies are held with 5,000 participants each; the dominant slogan at both is »Germany, united fatherland.«

Friday, December 15

In Berlin, a special Party Conference of the East German CDU, demanded by the membership, begins; its slogan is »Renewal and Future.« The 800 delegates represent roughly 140,000 Christian Democratic party members. Party Chairman Lothar de Maizière, who has held this position for only a few weeks, describes democratic centralism as the genetic defect of East Germany and the pseudo-socialism it practices. In his opinion, the word »socialism« has become hollow and has lost its usefulness. Winfried Wolk, former member of the main commission, resigns from the party. Wolk, a 48-year-old painter and graphic designer who has belonged to the CDU for 19 years, accuses the Party Conference of failing to deal sufficiently with its past. He says the country is facing disaster, but instead of yelling, people merely murmur. He adds that the CDU has long been the »SED's cudgel« rather than an independent party.

During a state visit to Prague, LDPD Party Chairman Manfred Gerlach declares that there will be no room in East Germany for neo-fascism or anti-Semitism. Where isolated incidents of this type occur, they are being met with all available means, including the state's legal weapons. He says no neo-fascist parties or organizations will be tolerated – that is, no branches of West Germany's so-called »Republikaner«.

Saturday, December 16

This is the start of a weekend of Party conferences at which the new and renewed forces will take stock and risk looking ahead. The first phase of revolutionary change seems to be completed. Old, static conditions have been shaken up and the groundwork laid for fundamental change. Now it is time to gather forces, draft convincing programs, and create majorities in order to introduce structural change that will reach to the roots of society in the coming elections.

At the final session of the CDU party Conference in Berlin, the party's newly-elected general secretary, Martin Kirchner, publicly admits his party's guilt, saying the perpetrators and victims had at the same time been victims and perpetrators.

Meanwhile, Democratic Awakening is meeting in Leipzig to found a party. Wolfgang Schnur, an attorney from Rostock, is chosen as its chairman. Gerald Wittenberg, a delegate from Erfurt, earns loud applause when he states that »the planned economy is dead, we don't want to resurrect that corpse, no more socialist experiments!«

At the second half of its special Party Conference in Berlin, the SED decides to regroup as the »Party of Democratic Socialism« and to operate under the double name »SED-PDS« until the next regular Party Conference. An earlier petition by radical reformers to dissolve the SED and form a new socialist party was rejected.

Criminal sociologist Wolfgang Brück, who has been observing the most recent activities of the right-wing radical »scene« in East Germany, gives his assessment: »I suspect that we will soon have to expect the organized emergence of a right-wing extremist organization from the darkness. There are considerable right-wing extremist views in East Germany.«

In the evening, rapid unification with West Germany is again demanded at a rally in Plauen attended by 10,000 people.

Sunday, December 17

West German and East German pollsters conduct a representative survey among East Germans with the following outcome: Seventy-one percent support the idea of socialism and 73% advocate a sovereign East Germany; only 27% call for a joint state with West Germany. Thirty-nine percent consider the West German economic system to be desirable; 61% would prefer »a thoroughly reformed socialist economic system.« »If elections were held tomorrow,« 86% would go to the polls. Of the 48% decided voters, 14% would vote SED, 9% SDP, 56% New Forum, 5% LDPD, 5% DCU, 3% the Greens, 3% the Peasants' Party (DBD), 1% Democratic Awakening and 1% NDPD.

Monday, December 18

During the second meeting of the Round Table, the government announces its decision to replace the Office of National Security, which is being dissolved, with a foreign and a domestic secret service. This leads to protests by opposition groups, who demand universal elimination of secret service agencies.

The governing West German parties CDU and CSU announce their desire to work formally with the East German CDU and support it in the coming electoral campaign. At the close of a conference in Frankfurt am Main of CDU parliamentary party chiefs from West Germany, delegates explain that it is the only party that uncompromisingly supports German unity.

The two German states agree to exchange agents held in each other's prisons. Twenty-five western spies are in custody in East Germany, and four East Germans are being held in the West.

The government spokesman in Bonn, Dieter Vogel, warns the East

December 18: The traditional Leipzig Monday demonstrations come to an end. People bring candles and stand in silence to honor the victims of Stalinism. (photo by Gerhard Gäbler)

against exaggerated expectations, saying »The Chancellor is not coming with a sack full of Christmas presents.« He is thereby dismissing hopes of a ten-year, 100 billion mark program for East Germany from the West German economy, which would have to be secured by the Bonn government.

In the evening, 100,000 demonstrators gather in Leipzig for a »silent close« to the demonstrations of autumn 1989 and in memory of the victims of Stalinism. There are few posters or banners. All the cities' church bells peal.

Tuesday, December 19

Although only a short time ago three-quarters of all East Germans surveyed opposed rapid unification with West Germany, West German Chancellor Helmut Kohl rides a wave of enthusiasm during a visit to Dresden. He is received at his hotel with cries of »Helmut, Helmut!« and »Germany, united fatherland!« He declares himself »very satisfied« after talks with East German Premier Hans Modrow. At a press conference, the two politicians announce the results of their talks: the Brandenburg Gate in Berlin will be opened before Christmas, and travel will be free for West Germans starting on Christmas Eve. All political prisoners will be released by Christmas. Modrow mentions that a »Treaty on Cooperation and Good Neighborliness« will be drafted, in order to gradually develop a treaty partnership with West Germany.

Unlike Oskar Lafontaine, the SPD leader of the Saarland, the Chairman of the German Social Democratic Party, Willy Brandt, expressly welcomes the growing »unity from below.«

Medical care in East Germany is in a precarious state because so many doctors have moved from the East to the West. The East Berlin governing council, the Magistrat, therefore offers young, unemployed West German doctors jobs and specialized training. West Berlin's governing council, the Senat, announces the shipment of 30 tons of medical supplies as part of a program of immediate assistance to the East Berlin health system.

Schleswig-Holstein becomes the first West German state to relax guidelines for travel to East Germany by civil servants. Minister of the Interior Hans Peter Bull explains that people with access to confidential information need only inform their employers in advance of such trips. Even state officials with security clearance at the »secret« and »top secret« levels may now travel to the East. However, such visits continue to be forbidden to employees of the domestic secret service and similarly-placed employees of the criminal investigation division of the police.

Wednesday, December 20

The consumer advice center of North Rhine-Westphalia has developed a new information packet to prevent East German immigrants from being victimized by fraudulent insurance agents and »credit sharks« even while still in reception centers and immigrant dormitories.

Former East German Undersecretary Alexander Schalck-Golodkowski apparently assisted the Swedish weapons manufacturer Nobel Kemi in illegally exporting weapons to Iran. Because of this suspicion, according to the Stockholm newspaper *Dagens Nyheter*, Swedish customs officials have requested permission from West German authorities to interrogate the East German politician, who is in custody in West Berlin. As an Undersecretary in the East German Ministry of Foreign Trade, Schalck-Golodkowski was also in charge of the arms trade.

For the first time, five leading West Berlin police officials meet with high-level representatives of the East German People's Police on the eastern side of the city. A central subject of the exchange of views, »after 41 years of silence,« is the impending opening of the Brandenburg Gate. Since the fall of the Berlin Wall, security issues have generally been dealt with by phone.

Two-time Olympic ice skating champion Katarina Witt, of Karl-Marx-Stadt, returns the 1988 »Bambi« prize awarded her by the West German publisher Burda. She has been repeatedly attacked in its publications in recent days for her former »closeness to the regime.«

Thursday, December 21

Following his trip to East Germany, Chancellor Helmut Kohl goes before the upper chamber of parliament, the Bundesrat, to advocate unification, but also emphasizes, »We all know that we are only at the beginning of a long and difficult road. We know that we must tackle the tasks before us with caution, patience and perceptiveness. We know that solutions must always be sought and found in consideration of our neighbors in Europe and in mutual trust.«

In the first visit by the head of a Western power, French President Francois Mitterrand meets with East German Prime Minister Hans Modrow in East Berlin for a working breakfast. He is accompanied by prominent members of the economic community who are hoping for joint ventures in areas like aviation, rail transport, telecommunications, and the food industry. They hope to gain ground that has been lost to West Germany.

Buying and selling of real estate in East Germany continues to be subject to government control. The current legal situation prevents real estate speculation by foreigners, according to an article in the *Berliner Zeitung* newspaper titled »Western Brokers Wait at the Starting Gate.« The article explains that the law forbids purchase for speculative purposes; use of so-called »straw men« as fronts would not help, as permits may be revoked once they are granted.

Friday, December 22

The Brandenburg Gate in East Berlin is reopened, in a pouring rain, to great international media attention. The breakthrough of the wall on both sides of the Gate for two pedestrian crossings marks a symbolic end to Berlin's 28 years of division.

At its third session, the Round Table adopts a list of priorities for future cooperation between opposition groups and the government. These include elimination of the secret services.

In apparent justification of the planned creation of an intelligence agency in East Germany, counter-intelligence reports increased activity by the U.S. and West German secret services. Western leaders, they say, are urgently interested in current information in order to revise their »political strategies for Germany.«

In many cities, vigils and solidarity rallies are held this evening for the opposition in Romania, which has clashed seriously with security forces in the last few days.

Saturday, December 23

The New Forum citizens' movement calls on the government to offer former East Germans whose citizenship has been revoked a dignified restoration of that citizenship. This should also apply to people forced to give up their citizenship by heavy psychological pressure. New Forum says that the example set by these people, in particular, contributed significantly to the changes now being achieved.

Christmas, December 24 – 26

At midnight on December 24, the visa requirement and the minimum currency exchange for West Germans visiting the East are ended. Over the holidays, 380,000 West Germans and 760,000 West Berliners travel to the East, while over 2 million East Germans visit relatives and friends in the West.

In Oelsnitz, in southern East Germany, New Forum comes up with a new idea. To repay the hospitality of West Germans, the local press calls upon East Germans to make lodgings available for free. A thousand beds are immediately offered to visiting West Germans.

Undersecretary Walter Priesnitz of the Federal Ministry for Inner-German Affairs says, in answer to a question, that all political prisoners in East Germany who are originally from West Germany, including West Berlin, have been released as agreed upon.

A special concert by Leonard Bernstein is the major event on the first day of Christmas. Long lines form for tickets at East Berlin's Schauspielhaus concert hall. Huge walls of monitors broadcast the concert to the packed Gendarmenmarkt square outside. Bernstein conducts Beethoven's Ninth Symphony, spontaneously changing it from an »Ode to Joy« to an »Ode to Freedom.«

Wednesday, December 27

At the fourth meeting of the Round Table, delegates insist that the government refrain from creating any new intelligence agency before the elections on May 6. They also demand greater public oversight of the process of dismantling the Office of National Security, a process that has not been particularly transparent thus far.

The Liberal Democratic Party (LDPD) advocates allowing former owners of businesses that were forcibly nationalized in 1972 to buy back those businesses.

East Germany begins to participate in the flourishing trade in pieces of the Berlin Wall. Limex-Bau Export-Import, a foreign trade agency, takes over the sale of available original pieces, saying that revenues will be used exclusively for humanitarian purposes.

Thursday, December 28

Anti-Soviet and neo-Nazi graffiti is found at the Soviet War Memorial in the Treptow district of East Berlin. Eight stone sarcophagi in the memorial grove and the base of the crypt have been defaced by unknown sprayers with words like »Occupiers Out,« »National Community [a Nazi phrase], Not Class Struggle,« and »Nationalism for a Europe of Free Peoples.« The originators of the act are unknown.

The media reports on a growing number of bomb threats and public declarations of sympathy with the radical right-wing »Republikaner« party. The East German police are aware of roughly 1,100 people linked to crimes motivated by radical right sentiments.

A study by the Bavarian Ministry of Social Welfare on economic differences between East and West triggers debate. The study finds that an East German must work ten minutes for a half liter of beer, while a West German earns one in only three minutes. The time worked to pay for a women's dress is 31 hours and ten minutes in East Germany, but only four hours and 44 minutes in West Germany.

Friday, December 29

The Defense Ministry in East Berlin undertakes its first changes in structure and personnel. General Fritz Streletz, a member of the old guard, is replaced as chief of staff of the National People's Army [NVA] as of January 1, 1990 by the former chief of the behind-the-lines services, Lieutenant General Manfred Grätz. General Horst Brünner, head of the main political office of the NVA, has already retired from active duty, and his office has been dissolved.

The reputation of the SED-PDS among the public has apparently risen since the party's reorientation. Now 34% would vote for it, compared with only 31.5% in November. A supposedly representative survey by sociologists at the East Berlin Academy of Social Sciences also finds that confidence in the government of Prime Minister Modrow is relatively strong. According to 41.4% of those surveyed, political life is being democratized at a suitable pace, while 23.9% actually feel the process is taking place too rapidly. According to this survey, undertaken by a research institute with close ties to the SED, Modrow is liked by 59% of the respondents. In an analogous survey in November, the figure was around 42%.

Saturday, December 30

A hitherto secret agreement concluded in early December between the Council of Ministers and the Union of Employees of State Organs comes to light. According to the *Berliner Zeitung* newspaper, the agreement would provide so-called »interim benefit« to former employees of ministries and the government apparatus when they are transferred to new positions. Should their former institutions be downsized or eliminated, these people would have a right to the difference between their present and former average salaries for three years. This leads to extreme discontent among »workers in the national economy,« who consider it a continuation of unjustified privileges.

Sunday, December 31

»We want to do everything we can to improve the economic situation for people in East Germany rapidly and perceptibly. You should be able to feel comfortable in your homeland – in Mecklenburg and Thuringia, in Brandenburg, Saxony and Saxony-Anhalt,« says Chancellor Helmut Kohl in his New Year's address. »In my ten-point program for German unity, I have shown the way in which the German people can once again achieve unity in free self-determination. The acceptance of independent parties and free elections in East Germany is an important step down this road.«

Earlier, the chairmen of the East German Council of State, the Council of Ministers, and the People's Chamber issued a joint New Year's message stating, »The year 1989 that is now ending will go down in the history of our country as the year of the peaceful revolution. East

Germany needs further revolutionary changes ... Even with the complete opening of the borders with West Germany and West Berlin, no sellout of East Germany will be permitted. No monetary union is planned.«

In the evening, some 100,000 people come together on both sides of the Wall at the Brandenburg Gate to ring in the New Year together. Many people from all parts of the East and West have traveled for hours in order to be present at the »Night of Nights.« A unification mood prevails.

December 31: People from East and West meet at the Brandenburg Gate to ring in the New Year together.
(photo by Gerhard Gäbler)

January 1990

Monday, January 1

The party at the Brandenburg Gate begins to spin out of control around midnight. Several dozen people climb the gate, Berlin's 20-meter-high trademark, and scale the Quadriga sculpture at the top. There they rip apart the East German flag, with its hammer-and-compass emblem, and hoist the West German and blue European flags. They then destroy spotlights and break leaves off the victory goddess's copper wreath. An hour and a half after midnight, this »New Year of the Century« ends with a tragic accident. A video screen, whose light metal scaffold has also been scaled by numerous young people, collapses, injuring some fifty people on the eastern side of the Brandenburg Gate, some of them seriously. They are brought by ambulance to hospitals in East and West Berlin. However, a carpet of countless shattered glass bottles makes it difficult for the ambulances to leave the scene.

Around 7.30 a.m. on New Year's morning, a plea for help reaches the West German customs office in Duderstadt (Göttingen county) from East Germany: »The coal bunker in the barn in Zwinge is burning, can you help us?« This call for aid from the People's Police leads to the first inter-German firefighting operation since the building of the Wall.

Since the early hours of the new year, soldiers have been demonstrating in Beelitz for military reforms. They have left the barracks and refuse to return to quarters until direct talks have begun. Similar demonstrations by soldiers take place in Dresden and Leipzig.

Tuesday, January 2

Four days after taking office, the new President of Czechoslovakia, Vaclav Havel, makes his first foreign visit to both German states. He flies to Munich in the afternoon, following discussions in East Berlin. »We Europeans must thank East Germany for beginning to tear down one of the worst walls,« says Havel at the Brandenburg Gate. His answers to questions about German unity are cautious.

Prime Minister Hans Modrow receives several Round Table delegates, saying the government seeks and needs advice. He reiterates his willingness to cooperate. »If we do not succeed in creating a climate of mutual respect, a climate of confidence-building,« the Premier emphasizes, »we will not have the necessary climate for free, democratic elections on May 6.« New Forum, which does not participate in this »closed-door session,« conditions its further participation in Round Table talks on the government response to questions that remain open. They see the Modrow cabinet as merely an interim government with limited authority, pending the first free elections.

The East German border and the Wall in Berlin will not last, according to Council of State Chairman Manfred Gerlach, and agreement is needed on new forms. Simple border demarcations are conceivable, like those used between many other countries.

The railroads are nearly strangled by the volume of returning traffic following the holidays. Travelers clamber through the windows of railroad cars, since platforms and corridors are hopelessly jammed. To keep departures from being delayed even further, railroad police are forced to intervene and physically prevent people from pushing their way through the doors.

Wednesday, January 3

Representatives of 16 parties, political groups and organizations come together in East Berlin for the fifth session of the Round Table. It is decided that the government must submit draft laws for the first half of 1990 to the Round Table delegates within a few days. In a joint declaration, eight of the opposition groups at the Round Table protest the establishment of an intelligence agency and a domestic security service (a so-called »Office for the Protection of the Constitution«) and threaten to walk out. They succeed in ensuring the establishment of a working group on security to provide independent oversight of the process of dismantling the Office of National Security.

Economics Minister Christa Luft provides information on the country's new debts, for which she blames a reduced intake of hard currency in 1989. She calculates current debt to the West at over 20 billion US dollars, while accounts in Western banks amount to only between 7 and 9 billion dollars. The Economics Minister also reports increasing problems on the labor market, where 25,000 positions are available, as opposed to 50,000 former government employees in need of new jobs. She also says her Ministry has no plans to permit foreign businesses to obtain a majority share in East German enterprises in the future.

Despite the new regulations since the beginning of the year that permit exchange of one West German mark for three East German marks at East German banks, people continue to exchange privately and illegally. However, the former black market rate of 1:10 to 1:20 has clearly fallen, and is currently hovering at around 1:5.

Opinion polls published today show two percent of East German young people tending towards the extreme right. This trend is strongest in East Berlin, at 6%, followed by Leipzig and Erfurt. Studies, interviews and surveys indicate »rising xenophobia,« as well as »primitive anti-Communism« and »forms of anti-Semitism.«

Heinz Galinski, chairman of the Central Council of Jews in Germany, voices dismay at the increase in neo-Nazi and anti-Semitic incidents in East Germany. In a statement, he calls on the government, political parties and social groups to »take energetic countermeasures to deal as decisively as possible with these excesses.«

In the evening, 250,000 people respond to an SED-PDS call for a protest against the defacement of the Soviet War Memorial in Treptow, where unknown perpetrators scrawled anti-Soviet slogans. At the rally they demand the rapid creation of a new secret service. The opposition maintains that the demonstration is a campaign maneuver and articulates the suspicion that the graffiti was actually placed there by former Stasi members.

Thursday, January 4

The East German Council of Ministers decides to reexamine the controversial interim benefit provisions for former employees of the dismantled state security service. However, Government spokesman Wolfgang Meyer rejects demands that the government refrain from creating a domestic security agency, saying this would be an »irreparable« error, given the current neo-Nazi activities.

In contrast, at a national conference in Leipzig the Citizens' Committee for the Dismantling of the Stasi demands an end to all preparations for new secret services.

To prevent misuse of subsidized East German services by West Germans and West Berliners, the government adopts immediate measures to prevent large-scale orders, in particular, for laundries, dry cleaners, shoemakers and tailors by non-East German citizens. Such orders may now be made only upon presentation of an East German identity card.

At a meeting in East Berlin of the Round Table working group to draft a party and association law, controversy arises over publicizing the assets of the SED and the other four parties in parliament. They prefer to first reveal their assets at their individual party congresses, which for the SED-PDS would mean April, at the earliest.

For the first time, environmentalists from East and West Germany come together at the Schönberg garbage dump to protest the western practice of dumping trash in East Germany. The demonstrators block the entry and exit to the dump with banners and demand an immediate end to all garbage exports and a cleanup of the waste site.

Friday, January 5

Roughly 24,000 of the total of 85,000 full-time employees of the former State Security Service and its successor agency are to be laid off by the beginning of January, according to a report by the government commissioner for the dissolution of the Office of National Security. By the end of last year, the report continues, 364 of 2,000 former Stasi buildings had been be released for other uses.

At the close of their first national coordinating meeting in Leipzig, the district citizens' committees for the dismantling of the intelligence services MfS/AfNS demand an investigation of the SED-PDS for »anti-constitutional activities.« They say that the Stasi was not subject to parliamentary oversight and was decisive in shielding the SED apparatus from any democratic influences. In their view, all special telephones, telexes and radio links still in use by the SED-PDS should be immediately shut down and dismantled, and SED-PDS organizations separated from all enterprises and public and state institutions.

In Leipzig, SED-PDS offices are searched by the police, prosecutors and members of the local citizens' committee. The offices searched include those of the Department of Internal Security of the district administration and rooms in an additional party building. Files and archives are sealed.

In Wolgast, on the Baltic coast, a group of neo-Nazis goes on trial for forming a »Secret SS Organization« with its own statute. Members held »SS ranks« and were stockpiling hunting weapons.

After more than two decades during which the text of the East German national anthem could not be sung, radio and television once again broadcast the original version, with the text by Johannes R. Becher: »Arisen from ruins/And facing the future/Let us serve you for the good/Germany, united fatherland.«

The wave of emigrants from East to West Germany continues. Each week, roughly 4,000 people switch countries. The West German Federal Ministry of the Interior announces today that 343,854 people emigrated from East Germany in 1989. They are attracted, among other things, by a variety of integration assistance benefits. But in a campaign speech in his home state, the leader of Saarland, Oskar Lafontaine (SPD), calls for the elimination of privileges for East Germans who emigrate to the West.

Saturday, January 6

Economist Bodo Thöns proposes creating a socialist stock market in East Germany. He believes distribution of stocks to employees offers a chance for all those involved in production to begin to feel like owners of the socialist economy. The chairman of the West German CDU Welfare Committee, Ulf Fink, also suggests the issue to East Germans of »people's stocks« from East German enterprises. He says that employees would become more involved if they could share in the profits as co-owners.

Sunday, January 7

At the close of a two-day conference of delegates, New Forum decides not to transform itself into a party, but instead to continue working as a decentralized civic movement. For now, this removes the threat of a feared split of New Forum, with its more than 200,000 members. Those members who had, at the beginning of the year, called for the formation of a German Forum Party did not attend the conference, but merely sent a message of greeting. The delegates decide to leave the Round Table if the government begins to establish a new secret service before the elections on May 6.

The Social Democrats in East Germany call for a nationwide demonstration against continued SED-PDS dominance this coming Sunday.

In a declaration, the SPD executive board maintains that the SED apparatus is preventing the country's democratization to a frightening degree.

Tens of thousands of people from East and West form a 60-kilometer human chain between the East German region of Eichsfeld and the Werraland in Lower Saxony and Hesse (West Germany). During the fifteen-minute action, they demand rapid changes in East Germany on the road to German unity.

Monday, January 8

The Round Table meets for the sixth time in an atmosphere of continued tension between government and opposition. The delegates from the civic movements request information from the government about a telex originating with the district authorities of the Office of National Security in Gera that called for the opposition to be shut down. Round Table delegates voice concern that the 60,000 employees of the Office of National Security are working against the democratization process.

In the afternoon, the opposition interrupts the talks at the Round Table with a statement of »no confidence« in the government commissioners for the dissolution of the Office of National Security, Peter Koch and Walter Halbritter. Neither, they say, is capable of answering the questions put to them on security policy and the dismantling of the Office. Markus Meckel of the SDP calls the government's behavior »shameless« and expresses serious doubts as to its willingness to change. He is applauded when he says, »The opposition must now organize new pressure on the streets, with warning strikes and demonstrations.«

The General Secretary of the West German CDU, Volker Rühe, calls on the East-CDU to leave the government. »The CDU in East Germany should now close the book on the SED and take the side of the opposition.«

Following a three-week intermission, tens of thousands resume the traditional Monday demonstrations in Leipzig. Their composition has changed visibly, and is made up almost solely of supporters of German unity, with their banners and black-red-gold flags. Demonstrations also take place in Karl-Marx-Stadt, Cottbus, Schwerin and other cities, with participants demanding information on SED party assets and opposing the three-year interim benefit provisions for Stasi employees. In Suhl and East Berlin, warning strikes are held in protest against these high interim payments.

Tuesday, January 9

The government gives in; former Stasi employees will now receive interim payments for a year at most, and only if they cannot find new jobs.

Egon Krenz (SED-PDS) gives up his parliamentary seat. In a statement, the 52-year-old Krenz explains that he is leaving parliament at the request of his Party leaders.

Former Undersecretary Alexander Schalck-Golodkowski, age 57, is released from investigative detention in West Berlin. State prosecutor Dietrich Schulz refuses to honor an extradition request from the East German authorities, saying there is insufficient evidence to support legal action.

In the view of SPD Deputy Chairman Oskar Lafontaine, the West German government should wait until after the May 6 elections before concluding an inter-German treaty. Such a decisive »constitutive act« should not be entered into with the present government, but only with one that is freely elected.

At a rally in Halle, several thousand craftspeople threaten a day-long strike if the government continues to ignore their needs. They demand unrestricted development of a private, small and medium-sized business sector. The demonstration, under the historic flags of the guilds, is the first of its kind in East Germany.

In several other towns, including Nordhausen (12,000) and Meiningen (10,000), demonstrators demand complete disempowerment of the SED and the dissolution of the secret services.

Wednesday, January 10

Defense forces claim to have exposed a U.S. spy probe near a »complex camp« of the National People's Army in the Karl-Marx-Stadt district. The device is presented to the public, to great media attention, by representatives of the domestic security service, which is still being built up, and the district police.

Former state and Party head Erich Honecker undergoes an operation for a malignant kidney tumor at the Charité hospital in East Berlin. The operating doctor accuses Honecker's personal physician of negligence, saying that the tumor could have been diagnosed in August, but was left untreated; instead, Honecker's intestine was operated on. Since then, the tumor has been able to grow unchecked; its full extent was discovered only during an examination to determine his fitness to be kept in custody.

Criminal law professor Hans Weber of Potsdam characterizes East Germany as a »land of many prisoners.« He contends that the country has one of the world's highest ratios of prisoners to population. Its prisons hold nearly as many inmates as West Germany's; yet East German crime statistics indicate only 120,000 crimes per year, while West Germany's show over 4 million. In addition, prison sentences in East Germany are longer overall. Weber traces this relationship to a »punishment fetish« that spread in the early 1970s as a result of a »one-sided defense and security mentality.«

According to a report in *Horizont* magazine, 177,500 foreigners live in East Germany. Of these, 43,033 hold permanent residency and 134,525 a long-term residency permit. The large majority came on the basis of government treaties that allowed them to work in an enterprise for four or five years. Ninety-four thousand foreign workers are employed in almost 1,000 factories. Sixty thousand are from Vietnam, 16,000 from Mozambique, 9,000 from Cuba, 7,000 from Poland and 1,000 each from Angola and China.

In the evening, demonstrations are held in more than 15 cities. Their main concern is taking away the power of the SED-PDS, which, despite all protests, continues to plan new secret services. In Berlin, New Forum calls for a protest rally on January 15 in front of Stasi headquarters, at which the entrance will be symbolically walled shut – assuming the secret police has not been shut down by then.

Thursday, January 11

According to Prime Minister Modrow, reunification of the two German states is not on the agenda. In a one-and-a-half-hour government statement before the People's Chamber in East Berlin, he says the relationship between East and West Germany can only be embedded in a European process. He condemns attempts to question his government's legitimacy and opposes an opposition veto power. To the applause of many members, Modrow points out that he did not become Prime Minister through a coup d'état. He stands by plans to create a domestic security service.

The legislative commission to draft a media law presents a draft bill that eliminates all media censorship. It grants natural and legal persons the right to publish newspapers, magazines and other publications; radio, television and the East German news agency ADN would become independent institutions. The licensing process for print media, hitherto controlled by the SED, would be eliminated, as would the licensing requirements for distributors of film, television and radio.

West Berlin attorney Peter Danckert, lawyer to former SED hard currency procurer Alexander Schalck-Golodkowski, says in an interview that his client will not return to East Germany. »It is out of the question, given the current situation in East Germany,« he says. »This approaches lynch justice.«

At the close of the parliamentary session, some 20,000 people protest this evening against government plans to create an intelligence agency and a domestic security agency. They form a human chain around the parliament building. Demonstrators in Erfurt and Gera protest payment of high interim unemployment benefits to former Stasi employees. The government's credibility and willingness to reform are questioned.

Friday, January 12

The second day of the parliamentary session is accompanied by demonstrations at the Palace of the Republic in East Berlin, at which thousands protest the continuing hegemony of the SED. Hundreds of taxis surround the building, honking and preventing access. Drivers are protesting manipulation of the electoral campaign and the privileges granted former Stasi employees.

Klaus Umlauf, of the Central Executive Board of the Union of Employees of State Organs and the Communal Economy, reports that the controversial interim benefits for ex-functionaries amount to 300 East German marks at most, and that this is currently being paid out to around 7,000 of approximately 20,000 former employees of central and local organs of the state. He says the funds come from the governing apparatus from money saved on salaries, not from enterprises in which the »dismissed employees« are now working. He adds that the law does not apply to members of the Office of National Security.

Prime Minister Modrow accedes to public pressure, agreeing to refrain from establishing a new secret service until after the elections and revoking the agreement to pay interim benefits to former Stasi employees. He says the dismantling of the Office of National Security will be accelerated and should be completed by June 30.

With the two-thirds majority required for a constitutional amendment, the People's Chamber adopts an investment protection law that will permit foreign investment in businesses in East Germany. However, the permitted share is limited to a maximum of 49%.

Saturday, January 13

For the first time, West German politicians publicly advocate a »German-German economic and monetary union« as the speediest means to achieve German unity even before the clarification of political unification, as the latter is dependent upon many unresolved foreign policy issues. According to Erich Riedl (CSU), Parliamentary Undersecretary in the West German Federal Ministry of the Economy, the goal should be a gradual, clearly defined growing together of the two economies. Matthias Wissmann, the parliamentary expert on economic policy for the CDU/CSU, recommends officially permitting the West German mark to function as a parallel currency. He says this must be followed immediately by radical price reforms, so that, as the next step, the West German mark can be officially introduced as a common currency.

Thousands of parents storm the department stores this Saturday morning to stockpile children's items before the price increases slated to go into effect on Monday. Mothers and fathers wait for hours on long lines to enter children's shoe and sweater departments. At the beginning of the coming week, prices for highly subsidized children's items will rise two to threefold.

Prime Minister Modrow suggests closer cooperation with opposition representatives and offers Ibrahim Böhme, the SDP manager, a position as Deputy Minister of the Environment.

The first conference of delegates of the Social Democratic Party in East Germany (SDP) in East Berlin decides, by an overwhelming majority, to adopt the name SPD for the party. In this way, it acknowledges its links to the SPD, dissolved in 1946 after the founding of the SED, and its connections to its West German sister party. The name change also clears the way for claims to former SPD party assets taken over in 1946 by the SED.

Demonstrations take place this evening in 15 cities against the attempt by the SED-PDS to reclaim its power. Forty thousand people gather in Plauen alone.

Sunday, January 14

SPD manager Ibrahim Böhme rejects Prime Minister Hans Modrow's offer to enter his cabinet as Deputy Environment Minister, saying it »is not serious.« Other representatives of new parties and groupings have already declared earlier that they will not participate in an SED-led government and administer crises for which they are not responsible.

The SED-PDS will transfer a portion of its party assets to the public treasury and limit its controlling position in the media. Among other things, the Party Presidium suggests turning 11 of 16 newspaper publishers and 21 of 26 printing facilities belonging to the SED-PDS into public property. The concentration of media in the hands of the SED-PDS is seen by opposition groups as placing crucial limitations on their own work.

In Berlin, members of citizens' committees to dismantle the state security service from various East German districts meet and resolve to »inspect« the still-active Stasi headquarters in the Lichtenberg district of Berlin in the next few days.

Tens of thousands demonstrate during the day against the continuing power of the SED-PDS. »The so-called *Wende* has absolutely not yet happened,« declares a representative of New Forum in Magdeburg, where 15,000 people take to the streets. He accuses the SED of a »policy of restoration,« which is especially clear in the reluctant dissolution of the security service. Twenty thousand people march through Görlitz carrying signs saying »Down with the SED« and »Get rid of the monopoly of power.«

Monday, January 15

According to the West German Ministry of the Interior, in the first two weeks of the new year alone, 20,818 East Germans have reported to West German authorities that they wish to remain in the West for good. At the same time, Bavaria's Minister of Social Welfare, Glück, says that emigrants from East Germany will no longer receive compensation for property or household items left behind. An East German regulation now permits emigrants complete control of the property they leave, so there is no longer any pressure to surrender one's assets.

During the seventh session of the Round Table, the government reports on the status of the dismantling of the state security service. The comprehensive system of mail and telephone surveillance has been shut down. Of 85,000 employees, 1,052 were active in telephone surveillance and 2,100 in mail surveillance. Five thousand worked in surveillance and investigation. Last year, 3.6 billion marks (1.3% of the budget) were set aside for the Stasi. Thirty thousand former Stasi employees have been dismissed since the dissolution of the service; an additional 22,500 persons will be integrated into the economy, health service, army and police.

Of the remaining 32,500 people, 20,000 will be dismissed in the immediate future. Twelve thousand five hundred employees are to be kept on until the final transfer of Stasi buildings to the state.

The citizens' committees that are overseeing the dismantling of the Stasi contradict this presentation. To their knowledge, for example, the Stasi headquarters in Berlin is still completely functional. Because the central office has its own structures throughout East Germany, it would be possible to reorganize the service, even though it is otherwise subject to extensive supervision. For this reason, the citizens' committees urge that Stasi buildings be supervised by the police and civic groups, and that the public prosecutor seal all offices, as has happened in local administrations.

Around 5 p.m., following New Forum's appeal, several thousand people gather at the former Ministry for State Security on Ruschestrasse in the Lichtenberg district of Berlin to protest the secret service's continuing operation. One entryway is symbolically walled shut, although members of the citizens' committee are meanwhile negotiating with Stasi officers inside for a peaceful transfer. There are loud protests and drumming on the gates, which are suddenly opened from within. Roughly 2,000 demonstrators thereupon push their way into the building; they are directed toward the supply section, which is then partially destroyed. Files and pictures of Honecker fly out of the shattered windows, and fire extinguishers are emptied.

In a dramatic appeal this evening, the government calls upon the public to remain calm »in this difficult hour.« The young democracy is in »great danger,« according to a declaration for which East German television interrupts its programming. Shortly before 7 p.m., Prime Minister Modrow, who has hurried there from the Round Table, urges the outraged crowd by loudspeaker to remain calm. Members of New Forum finally take the initiative, blocking the entryways and holding up signs reading »No violence.« After an hour or so, the intruders slowly leave the building.

Tuesday, January 16

The storming of the Stasi headquarters the evening before has changed the climate in the country and is an object of public concern. Dieter Winderlich, chief of the People's Police and Deputy Minister of the Interior, maintains there was a danger the violence would spread to the rest of the country. Since mass demonstrations were taking place simultaneously in twelve cities, events in Berlin might have had the »effect of a signal.«

The opposition distances itself from the violent storming of the East Berlin Stasi headquarters. Spokespeople from New Forum, the SPD and Democracy Now appeal urgently to the public not to let their understandable rage spill over into violence.

In Bonn, Chancellor Helmut Kohl retreats from his December 19 promise in Dresden to negotiate a cooperation treaty with the current East German government. He now says he will negotiate with a new government following the impending free elections.

Demonstrations in 12 towns, including several at Stasi offices, are peaceful.

Wednesday, January 17

Thirteen new parties have now emerged in East Germany and 154 associations have been registered with the government, according to Gotthard Hubrich, an official of the Ministry of the Interior. Another

113 associations are operating »on the basis of legal provisions,« for example in the health system and the field of culture. The Ministry of the Interior receives two to three applications from new organizations every day.

Inmates of the Karl-Marx-Stadt prison go on an indefinite strike, demanding to be included in the amnesty announced before Christmas. All inmates, except those employed in supply functions, have stopped working. The strikers demand the same rights for all prisoners in the country.

Warning strikes against SED-PDS attempts at a restoration take place in more than ten towns. Demonstrations are held in over 20 towns, with the interim benefits for former Stasi members – even though they have now been eliminated – continuing to generate the most anger.

Thursday, January 18

At the eighth meeting of the Round Table, opposition parties succeed in obtaining a right to speak in parliament. In addition, a resolution is adopted forbidding any media censorship and guaranteeing unlimited freedom of opinion to all citizens, along with free access to information. A media supervisory council will be established, to include representatives of all parties and groups participating in the Round Table.

Chancellor Helmut Kohl suggests bringing forward the People's Chamber elections planned for May 6, saying the Modrow government is rapidly losing the public's confidence. Government sources in Bonn also let it be known that such a step could be accelerated if the East German CDU were to leave the government.

A »Union of Victims of Stalinism« (BSV) forms in Berlin, demanding comprehensive rehabilitation of all victims and punishment of all perpetrators.

Some 2,500 watchdogs that once guarded the East German border with West Germany will be »resettled« in West Germany in the coming days and weeks, according to the German Animal Protection Society. No private owners could be found for the dogs in East Germany. These German Shepherds and Rottweilers are in perfect health and supposedly very friendly.

Numerous large demonstrations take place this evening, for example in Erfurt (40,000), Gera (30,000), and Rostock (15,000); protesters demand disempowerment of the SED-PDS, consistent dismantling of all Stasi units, and rapid German unity.

Friday, January 19

In Frankfurt on the Oder, ambulance drivers stop work in a three-hour warning strike to reinforce their demands for higher pay and better working conditions. In Suhl, bus and taxi drivers bring public transportation to a complete standstill in a warning strike for higher wages.

Professor Johannes Welcker of the University of Saarbrücken advises the government in East Berlin to immediately implement a convertible East German mark. In his view, this would fill store shelves »within a week,« even though these products might seem expensive at first. At the same time, it would bring movement to the state-prescribed wage and price system and force enterprises to adapt immediately to international competition.

In December, customs agents initiated over 5,600 criminal proceedings for violations of import and export regulations. Goods valued at 1.4 million East German marks and currency worth approximately one million East German marks have been confiscated. It is also reported that customs investigators handled 52 investigations in the same period, involving damages of 8.7 billion marks and concerning export of prohibited items such as shoes, children's textiles, baking ingredients and vegetables, the illegal export of East German marks, import of consumer electronics »for speculative purposes,« and smuggling out of cultural treasures and antiques.

Saturday, January 20

With the East German CDU's decision to remain in the government of Prime Minister Hans Modrow, a public debate flares up in the Bonn CDU/CSU on whether to continue cooperation with the East German party. CDU General Secretary Volker Rühe and CSU Chairman Theo Waigel distance themselves sharply from their East German sister party, while Deputy Party Chief Heiner Geißler and West Berlin CDU Chairman Eberhard Diepgen would continue cooperating.

In Leipzig, twelve Christian, liberal and conservative groups found the »German Social Union« (DSU). Leipzig Pastor Hans-Wilhelm Ebeling is elected chairman. The party supports rapid German unification and sees itself as a sister party to the Christian Social Union and Christian Democratic Union in West Germany.

Exactly 28 years, five months and seven days after August 13, 1961 – the day it was erected – East Germany officially begins to sell off the Berlin Wall. The foreign trade firm »Limex-Bau Export-Import« is responsible for »marketing the Wall« according to supply and demand criteria.

In Plauen, some 35,000 people demonstrate for the dissolution of the governing SED-PDS and better environmental conditions in the region. Several parties – including the SPD and the Green Party – present their electoral platforms during the rally. In 20 other towns, including Finsterwalde (15,000), Neubrandenburg (10,000), Greiz (8,000), and Berlin (5,000), a main issue, in addition to political demands, has become an improvement in working and living conditions in industrial enterprises, agriculture, and the health system.

Sunday, January 21

The crisis in the SED-PDS, in which various factions have meanwhile formed, takes a dramatic turn. The deputy Party Chairman and popular Mayor of Dresden, Wolfgang Berghofer, and 39 other party members declare their resignation from party. In a statement by the forty distributed this evening, they say they support a more »social democratic« program. Like other reformers, Berghofer and the other ex-members call for dissolution of the SED-PDS.

The opposition group Democratic Awakening, which transformed itself into a party a few weeks ago, hopes to join with »anti-socialist, Christian, liberal, social and conservative forces« for the elections on May 6. At the founding of the Thuringian state section, Chairman Wolfgang Schnur calls for a »strong electoral alliance of the political center«. The party renews its support for German unity and the introduction of a social-ecological market economy.

The Democracy Now (DJ) movement is the only one to resist the general trend toward reunification. At the close of its first state congress, the delegates emphasize in a statement that they reject »reunification in the form of exclusion« as well as »all attempts to implement or force immediate unity«. They advocate that the two states come together gradually through a three-stage plan leading to a demilitarized Germany.

Monday, January 22

At the ninth Round Table session in East Berlin, Prime Minister Hans Modrow offers ministerial posts to opposition members. He asks them to provide proposals for participation in the government as soon as possible, and says he hopes to hold coalition talks as soon as this week and to agree on a Grand Coalition in the coming weeks.

SPD Manager Ibrahim Böhme confirms that the opposition is willing, in this »emergency situation,« to enter the government without long coalition negotiations.

Defense Minister Theodor Hoffmann highlights the loyalty of the National People's Army »to the democratic revolution in East Germany« and to the Modrow government. The background to this is a newspaper report on preparations for a putsch by former Stasi members and the army, which is decisively rejected by all participants at the Round Table.

According to Foreign Minister Oskar Fischer (SED-PDS), the Modrow government is continuing its efforts to conclude a treaty with West Germany on cooperation and good neighborly relations. The treaty community striven for here can later be expanded into a confederation. He says there is no opposition abroad to a pan-European confederation, in which both German states can grow together into a single German polity.

In a visit to East Berlin, British Foreign Secretary Douglas Hurd emphasizes that Great Britain will always support »the Germans' right to free self-determination.« »The relationship between the two German states must be decided by the Germans themselves in a free, democratic way,« he says during a visit to East Germany lasting several days.

The State Office for Nuclear Security and Radiation Protection confirms to the Ministry of the Environment in Bonn a report in *Der Spiegel* magazine that East Germany came close to nuclear disaster in 1976. At the nuclear plant near Greifswald, a single emergency unit barely prevented a meltdown of the core following a fire in the power grid and the failure of eleven pumps. Environment Minister Klaus Töpfer was not told about this near-disaster during a visit last week.

More and more West Germans now support German unification and expect it to occur soon. Seventy-four percent of those surveyed in January advocate reunification, while 14% oppose it. Sixty-eight percent expect such a development in ten years, at most. The controversial visit to Bonn by Prime Minister Modrow in early February is welcomed by 73.5% of West Germans.

In Leipzig, over 100,000 people demonstrate this evening for rapid unification of both German states and an end to the power of the SED-PDS. According to the ADN news agency, a »regular hunt« ensues against a group of young leftists who call attention to themselves with chants, banners and East German flags. They are forced to hide in the cafeteria of Karl Marx University.

Demonstrations are also reported in Dresden (80,000), Karl-Marx-Stadt (60,000), Zwickau and Halle (20,000 each), Aue and Magdeburg (15,000 each), Suhl (10,000), and 25 other towns.

Tuesday, January 23

There are currently as many as 85,000 unemployed East Germans, according to Werner Peplowski of the trade union association FDGB. He calls on the government to plan a special fund to support the unemployed as part of the national budget.

The almost five-meter-high symbol of the Socialist Unity Party of Germany, the two shaking hands that can be seen from afar on the facade of the SED-PDS party headquarters on Werderscher Markt in East Berlin, is taken down. This is evaluated by the media as a sign of the party's decreasing power.

The initial signatories of the »For our Country« appeal on November 28, 1989 take stock, saying that 1.16 million East Germans called for East Germany's continued independence. The signatories include the writers Christa Wolf, Stefan Heym and Volker Braun and Pastor Friedrich Schorlemmer.

In Berlin, thousands of craftsmen and small businesspeople demonstrate today for better opportunities for development, including easier access to materials and tools and lower taxes. Warning strikes for better working conditions occur in over 10 towns. Demonstrations against continued SED-PDS power and for rapid German unity also continue in numerous towns, with participant figures beween 20,000 (Nordhausen) and 1,000 (Weimar).

Wednesday, January 24

The Round Table working group on a new constitution takes stock for the first time and announces that it will adopt the principles of a new East German constitution by the end of March.

The complete collapse of the economy is foreseeable in one or two years if necessary raw materials cannot be imported due to lack of hard currency. Formerly popular exports will no longer be salable on the world market. This is the gloomy picture pained by Siegfried Schiller, deputy director of the Manfred von Ardenne research institute in Dresden. According to the professor, only western investment of 500 billion marks can help, and an additional 100 to 200 billion will be needed to resolve ecological problems.

In the textile workers' city of Limbach-Oberfrohna in the Saxon district of Karl-Marx-Stadt, with its roughly 30,000 residents, 15,000 demonstrators force the city council to resign. The local Round Table takes over the administration of government. Demonstrations and warning strikes also take place in some 20 other towns.

Thursday, January 25

The government decides to permit complete business freedom. Limitations on enterprise size and importation of tools and materials are rescinded.

The CDU pulls its ministers out of the government in order to open the way for negotiations with new parties and groups in the run-up to the elections.

At the city Round Table, Magdeburg's Mayor, Werner Nothe, demands that the SED-PDS immediately cease all political activities in the vicinity of the city of Magdeburg. Nothe himself belongs to the party and was a delegate to the special SED Party Conference in East Berlin in December. He believes the party should dissolve itself.

The guard dogs offered to West Germans are dangerous to inexperienced owners, according to the Association of German Shepherds. According to the organization, dogs like these, which have had little social contact with humans, are difficult to integrate into families when they are older and cannot really be retrained for normal everyday activity. The association says the German Animal Protection Society has done »a disservice« with its ad campaign for the roughly 2,500 retired East German guard dogs.

Twenty thousand people demonstrate in Erfurt for a complete end to the security police; in Gera, 15,000 call for the dissolution of the SED-PDS and a united Germany. Additional demonstrations and warning strikes take place in 25 towns.

Friday, January 26

Spokespeople for all parties and groups at the Round Table declare their willingness to take part in an interim government. Wolfgang Schnur, chairman of Democratic Awakening, speaks of the necessity of forming a government of national responsibility, including the SED-PDS, until the parliamentary elections on May 6.

Egon Bahr, member of the presidium of the West German SPD, appeals for a stable currency relationship between the two German states. Speaking before more than a thousand participants at a civic forum in Treffurt, East Germany, he says Bonn must guarantee such a relationship. In the town where he was born, Bahr cautions East Germans not to begin a »witch hunt« of SED members.

In Plauen, the district leadership of the SED-PDS ceases operations. It has lost many members in the past months and feels incapable of serious opposition to the massive local demands for German unity.

The first national, independent weekly paper in East Germany comes on the market. New Forum applied for a publishing license in December, and now – after a record preparation time of only a month – it brings out *die andere*. The sixteen-page newspaper, with a classic Berlin format, is led by chief editor Dietmar Halbhuber in »some sort of grass roots democratic« way, as he puts it in an editorial.

Saturday, January 27

At the official founding congress of New Forum in Berlin, the heretofore dominant left-wing faction is defeated in the program debate. Instead of anchoring the idea of two states in the organization's statement of principles, the delegates include a profession of belief in the unity of the German nation and in the gradual coming together of the two German states, with the modus of German unity to be decided in a plebiscite. Speaker Jens Reich states, »The romantic phase, the wild, Sturm-und-Drang period of our revolution is over.«

Former SED Politburo member Joachim Herrmann is arrested. He has been under investigation for high treason in connection »with his responsibility for the media policies of the past years, which violated basic rights,« according to the Prosecutor General's office. Arrest warrants are also issued for the former head of the State Planning Commission, Gerhard Schürer, who is accused of »criminal abuse of trust.«

During an election tour through East Germany, Willy Brandt speaks to 100,000 in Gotha and 35,000 in Eisenach, where he calls for a clear but cautious road to German unity.

Sunday, January 28

The Chairman of the East German CDU, Lothar de Maizière, responds cautiously to the insistence of the Chairman of the West German CSU, Theo Waigel, that he strongly attack the East German SPD now. »As a Christian, I prefer objectivity. West German politics should slow its tempo for us and give us time to think and to structure.« De Maizière, who is the deputy Prime Minister in Modrow's cabinet, demands extensive economic credits from West Germany.

Speaking in front of some 3,500 enthusiastic listeners in Magdeburg, East Germany, this evening, Ernst Albrecht, state leader of Lower Saxony, suggests rapid introduction of a unified German citizenship. He says the most important thing is to create »de facto«German unity. No one, he maintains, can prevent Germans from forming a legal unit and, for example, »step by step, making a German mark out of the West-mark and the East-mark.«

Monday, January 29

Former state and SED leader Erich Honecker is released from the hospital and immediately placed under arrest.

Prime Minister Hans Modrow announces that the national budget deficit has risen to 17 billion marks. The economic situation is worsening in worrisome fashion. Strikes have led to loss of production, and social tensions cannot be governed with the available political structures. Local administrations have largely disintegrated or are no long-

Demonstrators protest against the release of Erich Honecker from custody and demand and long prison sentence.
(photo by Johannes Beleites)

er capable of decision-making. Some councillors are no longer recognized. The rule of law and the legal system are increasingly being called into question. Therefore, early elections and a broad-based interim government are unavoidable.

The People's Chamber adopts a new election law that no longer forbids political parties and associations from accepting material and financial support from outside the country. The prohibition on such aid that was originally intended met with vehement public protest. In the parliamentary debate, it is proposed that elections be brought forward to March 18.

In the evening, some 100,000 residents of Leipzig gather for the traditional Monday demonstration. As in other rallies over the past weeks, the demonstration is marked by fury and indignation at the SED-PDS, successor to the former ruling party, and by the demand of a majority of participants for immediate unification of the two German states. On banners, March 18 is already welcomed as »liberation day.«

Tuesday, January 30

In a surprise statement during Prime Minister Modrow's visit to Moscow, Soviet Premier Mikhail Gorbachev declares that the principle of German unification will never be called into question by anyone. The two politicians are discussing issues concerning the shape of German unity. Gorbachev insists that a united Germany must remain neutral.

As a result of the talks, the SED-PDS leadership abandons its insistence on East German independence. In a statement, the party lends its support to the »commonality of the German nation and the two German states, which goes hand-in-hand with the unification of Europe and contributes effectively to it.«

In the view of economist Heinz-Dieter Haustein, East Germany is not facing a reform of its economy, but a change of economic systems. There is no historic precedent for this, he says, and researchers in East and West have no blueprint for turning a planned economy into a market economy. »We are living through a great adventure,« says Haustein. »We are pushing off from one shore, but do not know whether and when we will arrive on the other.«

Former East German leader Erich Honecker is released from custody this afternoon and brought to the church-run Lobetal rest home near

Bernau, north of Berlin. Honecker's lawyers say the former leader is suffering from »general depression.«

At a press conference, members of the citizens' committee working to dismantle the former Stasi headquarters on Normannenstrasse in East Berlin report at a press conference that they have found and secured twelve kilometers of files in the 60-building complex.

According to Kurt von Haaren, chairman of the West German Postal Workers' Union, the West German intelligence service, the BND, continues its surveillance of mail from East to West Germany for purposes of »strategic oversight.« Telephone conversations are also surveilled.

Wednesday, January 31

Prime Minister Hans Modrow's sensational statements on German unity in Moscow this morning are an attempt, according to the East German CDU, to jump on the bandwagon and coopt other parties' demands for unification.

The continuing, apparently unstoppable wave of emigrants from East to West Germany threatens to become a major national problem, according to the German Conference of Cities. If conditions are not stabilized as hoped, West Germany can expect as many as 850,000 to 1.5 million immigrants, says Manfred Rommel, President of the Conference and Mayor of Stuttgart, following a meeting of the Presidium in Speyer. The Conference of Cities demands limitations on the free choice of place of residence, in order to prevent immigrants from concentrating in large cities and already-overburdened states such as North Rhine-Westphalia. In addition, the Federal government should cease »subsidizing emigration and immigration,« says Rommel; emigration to West Germany should not »be made financially attractive as well.«

At evening demonstrations in more than 20 towns, protesters criticize the SED-PDS's media and technology edge in the election campaign and demand that SED-PDS property be turned into public property.

February 1990

Thursday, February 1

One of the most important achievements of the *Wende*, the »Law on Travel Abroad by Citizens of the German Democratic Republic,« officially comes into force. All citizens may now leave the country at any time, with a passport.

Upon his return from Moscow, Prime Minister Modrow presents to the astonished public his strategy for accomplishing German unity. »Germany will once again become the unified fatherland of all citizens of the German nation. Responsibility, caution, and an understanding of what is possible and what Europe can bear are necessary so that no danger to the life and property of its neighbors will ever again arise,« he tells the press in East Berlin. As conceivable steps, Modrow suggests a treaty community with confederative elements, creation of a confederation of East and West Germany with joint organs, transference of the rights of sovereignty of both states to confederate organs, and finally, elections to create a unified German state in the form of a German federation or a German union.

Responding to Modrow's most recent statement, Chancellery Minister Bohl in West Berlin states that West Germany will only negotiate on German unity with a freely-elected government after March 18. It goes without saying, he adds, that the path to unification must be an integral part of the overall process of European unity. However, that path cannot include a strategy of neutrality, which would contravene the logic of European unity.

Chancellor Helmut Kohl meets in West Berlin with CDU Chairman Lothar de Maizière to discuss formation of an electoral alliance of several conservative parties. The chairman of Democratic Awakening, Wolfgang Schnur, already invokes »a clear majority« that identifies with Christian, liberal, social and conservative values.

The government decides upon an immediate increase in wages and salaries for 2.3 million blue and white collar workers. The raise, which requires roughly 3.6 billion marks, will go into effect between March 1 and July 1. The Council of Ministers also adopts regulations on early retirement for older workers who have lost their jobs and on compensation payments while work is being sought. Both are sent to the Round Table.

The Vice-President of the East German Building Academy, Professor Werner Teuber, paints a merciless picture of the disastrous situation of East German housing. Of 7.1 million apartments, half a million have neither bath nor shower, and nearly a million have no toilet in the apartment. Roughly half of all apartments continue to be heated with coal stoves. Average building age is 58 years. Of the apartment buildings built before World War II, 11% are in such a state of disrepair that they are no longer salvageable.

Friday, February 2

SED-PDS chief Gregor Gysi meets in Moscow with Soviet leader Mikhail Gorbachev to discuss issues surrounding the unification process. It becomes clear that the Soviets have a vague idea of dissolving the military alliances and turning them into political ones, so that Germany does not become a member of NATO.

Modrow's concept of »Germany united fatherland« leads the United Left to rescind their participation in an all-party government, saying they will not be party to such policies.

From the opening of the borders on November 9 of last year until the end of January, the East German authorities have issued 12,275,354 visas for foreign travel. During the same period, 44,510 applications for emigration to West Germany and West Berlin were granted, 12,480 of them in January alone, according to the Ministry of the Interior. There have been difficulties in issuing new East German passports; 5,000 applications are made each day, and printers are working around the clock. Until the end of the year, East Germans may travel with their personal identity cards alone.

For the first time in East Germany, workers go on an unlimited strike. The personnel of the Thomas Müntzer potash works in Bischofferode, in the Erfurt district, are striking for an across-the-board 400-mark wage hike. The workers also say they hope to send a signal regarding the need to break out of outdated economic structures. The majority of profits should be reinvested within the enterprise, not paid to the state, they maintain.

Saturday, February 3

In an interview with the *Neues Deutschland* newspaper, Economics Minister Christa Luft says she is striving to achieve a stable exchange rate between the West German and East German marks. However, she says the rate must be supported by West Germany, and should permit convertibility by 1992; savings must retain their value.

The founding Congress of the Green League comes to an end in Schkopau. In the program it has adopted, the organization describes itself as a network and a non-partisan association interested only in East Germany's ecological reform, an expansion of nature protection laws, and stronger public oversight. Klaus Schlüter is given a mandate to participate in the Modrow government as a minister without portfolio.

Democratic Awakening begins its election campaign in East Germany with a rally in front of the Halle city hall. Speaking to 5,000 participants, Party Chairman Wolfgang Schnur, already calling himself the future prime minister, calls for an end to socialist experiments and introduction of an ecological market economy. The guest speaker, West German Minister of the Environment Klaus Töpfer (CDU), maintains that the parliamentary election must be a final rejection of socialism.

Demonstrations take place in 12 additional towns, including Plauen (30,000), Arnstadt (6,000), Finsterwalde (5,000), Potsdam (4,000), and Stralsund (3,000), with many demanding the resignation of the local administrations.

Sunday, February 4

The Chairman of the East German SPD, Ibrahim Böhme, accuses the CDU in Bonn of »intolerable interference« in the campaign. While CDU Chairman Helmut Kohl claimed only a few months ago to be interested in supporting all democratic forces, says Böhme, the CDU is now cooperating with the old East German CDU, which shared responsibility for the policies of former East Germany, to form a conservative alliance.

From now on, the SED-PDS will be called only the »Party of Democratic Socialism« (PDS) and will campaign under that name, the party's Executive Committee decides in East Berlin. It maintains that the PDS has eliminated its old leadership, given up its monopoly of power, broken with past structures and begun to deal with its history. It also decides to give three billion marks to the state. This money comes from a fund held outside of its official accounts that includes unused profits from party-owned enterprises over the past 20 years. A report on party finances indicates that the SED took in 1.6 billion marks and spent approximately 1.75 billion marks last year.

Monday, February 5

Parliament agrees to the formation of a »Government of National Responsibility« that would grant representatives of groups and parties at the Round Table positions as ministers without portfolio. Earlier, Premier Modrow urged parliament to approve the new governing constellation developed by the Round Table. He says the situation in the country has worsened since last week's parliamentary session, and East Germany can only be governed with broad responsibility.

Parliament agrees to bring the date of parliamentary elections forward to March 18. In a further resolution by the People's Chamber, activities by the far right »Republikaner« continue to be prohibited, and successor or substitute organizations with the same goals are also forbidden to become politically active in East Germany.

In West Berlin this evening, representatives of the three conservative parties Democratic Awakening (DA), the German Social Union (DSU), and the CDU, agree to run for parliament jointly on March 18 as the »Alliance for Germany.«

The striking miners at the Thomas Müntzer potash works in Bischofferode, in the southern Harz, are successful. Their demands for a 400-mark wage increase per employee and for the combine's economic independence are met.

Tuesday, February 6

If parliamentary elections were held now, the SPD would achieve a landslide with 54% of the votes, according to a representative survey. Assuming 80% voter participation, the PDS would receive 12%, the CDU 11%, New Forum 4%, and the LDPD 3% of the votes. According to this survey, all other parties and movements would receive less than 3%. Three of four people surveyed (76%) advocate unification of the two German states, with 38% calling for immediate unification but 43% opposed to rapid action.

In the words of Walter Momper, the SPD Mayor of West Berlin, German unification will not be unification of two equal countries, but an »annexation out of poverty.« The motives of East Germans are not national, but social and economic.

The Greens become the last party in the West German Bundestag to abandon their demand for preservation of two German states. »East Germans are now deciding what they want, and that's the way it should be. They want unification; we had good arguments for not wanting it. Now we have to live with it, that's all there is to it!« declares spokesman Udo Knapp. »It is high time for West Germans and us Greens to wake up.« He says unity will require a great deal from all West Germans.

Wednesday, February 7

The West German government agrees to the Chancellery's plan for rapid economic and monetary union with East Germany and forms a cabinet commission on German unity to accomplish it. The commission, composed of most of the ministers and chaired by Chancellor Helmut Kohl, will take the necessary preparatory steps.

The chairman of the conservative German Social Union (DSU) in East Germany, Hans-Wilhelm Ebeling, reminds the West of the need to aid his party. He says the Social Democrats' lead in East Germany could be narrowed »if people on the other side wake up and give us solid support.«

Newspapers report that despite Round Table objections, Chancellor Kohl plans six major events in East Germany during the election campaign. CDU General Secretary Volker Rühe will travel through all districts and provide active support to the Alliance for Germany.

The civic movements New Forum, Democracy Now and the Initiative for Peace and Human Rights agree in Berlin to form a joint »Alliance 90« and run a joint campaign for the March 18 elections.

Thursday, February 8

At the urging of the Round Table, the government decides to form a state »Committee for the Dismantling of the Former Office of National Security« to manage the practical task of dismantling the Stasi as a central depository. The Round Table's working group on security announces that the Stasi recorded data on six million East German citizens. The many files will be placed in district depots under the supervision of citizens' committees.

U.S. Secretary of State James Baker proposes major troop reductions in Central Europe if the Soviet Union reciprocates by agreeing to German unification; he says the modalities would be negotiated among the four World War II occupying powers and the two German states.

British Prime Minister Margaret Thatcher acknowledges for the first time that the forthcoming elections in East Germany »will probably lead to the reunification of Germany.« Speaking in the House of Commons in London, she calls for discussions as soon as possible of the necessary effects on NATO.

Israel's Deputy Foreign Minister, Benjamin Netanyahu, sees reunification of the two Germanies as unavoidable. Speaking in the Knesset in Jerusalem, he expresses the Israeli government's hopes that reunification will not once again bring forth a »murderous German nationalism.«

The chairman of the far right »Republikaner«, Franz Schönhuber, is once again denied permission to enter East Germany. Border guards stop him at the Berlin crossing point Checkpoint Charlie with the words, »You are an undesirable person in East Germany.«

Rudolf Stadermann, President of the East German Association of Entrepreneurs, announces East German plans to return 10,000 to 15,000 nationalized enterprises to their rightful owners over the next six months, in hopes of thus boosting the economy. The largely middle-sized enterprises were taken over by the state in 1972 in return for a small, mainly symbolic compensation.

Prime Minister Modrow informs his cabinet that he has not yet been officially informed of Bonn's latest decisions regarding a monetary union, and that he only knows what the media has reported. With the new cabinet members from opposition parties and groups, he discusses the introduction of unemployment benefits and an early retirement law to deal with rising unemployment.

Friday, February 9

In a letter to the World Jewish Congress, Prime Minister Hans Modrow for the first time accepts the responsibility of all Germans, including East Germans, for the genocide of the Jews.

The West German CDU announces the creation of effective campaign headquarters in all 15 East German districts, where members of West German CDU party organizations will work as full-time advisors. In the coming weeks, the party headquarters in Bonn will be turned into a »service center« for the »East German Alliance.«

Five weeks before the first free elections, half the population (51%) has decided upon a party, according to an INFAS survey. The SPD has a clear lead among decided voters, with 38%. Seven percent prefer the former SED (now PDS), 5% the CDU, and 3% the Peasants' Party (DBD). New Forum, Democratic Awakening, the LDPD and the NDPD would receive 1% each. The conservative Alliance did not yet exist at the time of the survey. The pollsters find a clear majority for unification of the two Germanies: 44% in West Germany and 41% in East Germany support rapid joinder, while 37% of East Germans and 31% of West Germans prefer the countries to grow together over the long term as part of a united Europe.

Saturday, February 10

During negotiations between Chancellor Kohl and Mikhail Gorbachev in Moscow, the Soviets voice concern over the extremely rapid process of unification of the two German states, saying a variety of foreign policy problems – such as integration in the military alliances – have not yet been resolved. Kohl suggests that expansion of NATO onto East German territory might not be necessary. At the same time, he offers the Soviet Union extensive economic aid.

The far-right »Republikaner« have formed a new state chapter in Brandenburg with members from East Germany, according to Party Chairman Franz Schönhuber. He says roughly 100 East Germans, mainly young people, took part in establishing the branch. Schönhuber announces that despite the ban placed on his party by the People's Chamber, it hopes to operate »everywhere in East Germany.«

At a reading in East Berlin, West German author Günter Grass calls for financial »compensation« for East Germany and appeals for a confederation of the two German states. Grass maintains that because East Germany bore the main brunt of the war, suffering wave after wave of dismantling and enjoying no Marshall Plan aid, West Germany is obligated to pay compensation to East Germany. He feels a tax increase of 3% would be a just way of taking East Germany out of the »position of supplicant.«

Sunday, February 11

Explaining the West German government's reluctance to deal with the East German cabinet under Hans Modrow, West German Minister of the Interior Wolfgang Schäuble says the East German government's plans have lacked »market economy consistency.« Greater clarity and decisiveness of reform are necessary, he maintains; socialism, which gave the collective priority over individual freedom, has »finally given up the ghost.« According to Schäuble, in addition to full civil rights and equal opportunity, it is time to introduce the social market economy and state unity.

At an extraordinary LDPD Party Congress in Dresden this weekend, university professor Rainer Ortleb is chosen as successor to Manfred Gerlach. At the same time, the party resolves to change its name to LDP. In the presence of the leaders of the West German Free Democratic Party (FDP), the delegates call for rapid merger of the two parties, as well as for strengthening of free entrepreneurship, rapid monetary union, and a unified state in the near future.

Following tough negotiations in Dresden, leaders of the LDP, FDP, and the German Forum Party agree on a liberal alliance for the March 18 parliamentary elections. It will be called the »Union of Free Democrats.«

Monday, February 12

At its twelfth session, the Round Table advocates a monetary union between the two German states in principle, but does not authorize Prime Minister Modrow to conclude such an agreement during his impending visit to Bonn; it rejects »premature surrender of East German financial sovereignty« and says it is crucial to agree upon a social welfare charter at the same time. Instead, the Round Table demands from the West German government a »solidarity contribution of 10 to 15 billion DM,« independent of any further negotiations, saying it is in West German interests to counteract a destabilization of East Germany.

The Social Democratic Mayor of West Berlin, Walter Momper, accuses the West German government of providing little concrete assistance to East Germans in the past weeks. He says that Bonn has »stood rather idly by while things go to pot.« East German citizens have seen little of the immediate aid promised by Helmut Kohl, he adds, and the lack of action by the West German government to deal with existing problems has contributed to the exodus from East Germany. Current stalling tactics and the government's conscious spreading of rumors of impending East German insolvency are irresponsible, says Momper, and only serve to further destabilize the country.

At the traditional Monday demonstration in Leipzig, the recently-formed Alliance for Germany distributes flyers with their electoral program for rapid German unity. The flyers are printed in West Germany. Howling groups of right-wing extremists attack information stands run by left-wing groups and burn their materials.

Tuesday, February 13

During an official visit to Bonn by an East German government delegation led by Prime Minister Hans Modrow, agreement is reached on the formation of a joint commission of experts to lay the groundwork for monetary union. However, the East German request for a West German solidarity contribution to boost the East German economy is rejected.

Hans Modrow points out that East Germany not only can contribute important intellectual and cultural values to a united Germany; it also has solid material value. The net national wealth of East Germany is 1.4 trillion marks, including national property of 980 billion marks and 6.2 million hectares of unencumbered agricultural land.

The foreign ministers of the four victorious World War II powers hold talks in Ottawa, during international disarmament negotiations, on ways of clarifying the external modalities of German unification with the two German states. »Two-Plus-Four Talks« are proposed with this purpose in mind.

A Media Supervisory Council is formed in East Berlin to guarantee freedom of opinion, information and the media. The institution was approved by the People's Chamber in early February, at the initiative of the Round Table. Members of the Council include delegates from the parties and organizations represented at the Round Table and from parliamentary parties.

Wednesday, February 14

Prime Minister Hans Modrow and his delegation return to East Berlin, disappointed at the outcome of the inter-German summit meeting. In a final meeting with Finance Minister Theo Waigel (CSU), Modrow still failed to extract a promise of immediate aid of 10 to 15 billion marks as requested by the Round Table. Most of the Round Table ministers who accompanied Modrow to Bonn are extremely critical of the West German government. Matthias Platzek (East German Greens) calls the behavior of Bonn politicians »schoolmasterish.« Other delegation members refer to a public snub. They say West Germany is apparently interested in lowering the costs of unification through economic caution and an exaggeratedly negative presentation of the situation in East Germany.

The council of experts in charge of evaluating West Germany's overall economic development, known as the »Five Wise Men,« voices its reservations about an inter-German monetary union. In a letter to Chancellor Helmut Kohl, the group describes the rapid introduction of the West German mark into East Germany as the »wrong means of stopping the stream of emigrants.«

The four victorious World War II powers and the two German states jointly state their intention to »create German unity.« At the close of an »open skies« conference of foreign ministers of NATO and the Warsaw Pact in Ottawa, the six countries agree to a conference of their six foreign ministers on »external aspects« of unification, including the »issue of the security of neighboring countries.«

Thursday, February 15

In the words of Chancellor Kohl, a future united Germany must not be neutralized or demilitarized, but must remain part of the Western alliance. Kohl describes West Germany's starting point for unifica-

Press conference with Hans Modrow and Helmut Kohl on the occasion of an official visit to Bonn by an East German government delegation. The hope for immediate financial aid has not been fulfilled.
(photo by Frank Darchinger)

tion, from an economic point of view, as »unusually favorable in many respects.« He refers to the country's foreign trade surpluses and the willingness to invest economically in East Germany. The problems of a new economic beginning in East Germany are »anything but simple, but are ultimately soluble and capable of being dealt with by a country like the Federal Republic.«

According to Government spokesman Wolfgang Meyer, East Germans' fear of a devaluation of their savings is unjustified. He calls the lines that have formed at banks and the mass withdrawals regrettable. Politicians in Bonn and elsewhere, as well as the media, have in his view been spreading rumors that stirred up these fears for savings.

The Democratic Awakening party, part of the Alliance for Germany, calls for immediate introduction of the D-mark into East Germany. However, the party says the public must be informed that a monetary union would lead temporarily to relatively high unemployment.

An unemployment association is formed in East Germany; its targets are all the unemployed and those »potentially threatened by planned economic and market mechanisms.« The Minister of Labor and Wages agrees to the association's creation. According to official statistics, there are already over 50,000 unemployed people in East Germany.

The opening of the inter-German border and political developments since the fall of the Berlin Wall have caused a significant rise in the price of East German postage stamps. Almost all complete East German collections are sold at a spring auction in West Berlin in early February.

Friday, February 16

The politicians' plan, born of necessity, to rapidly build up an economic and monetary union without a careful cost-benefit analysis continues to appear very bold to Central Bank President Karl-Otto Pöhl. He says that West Germany will need to invest billions to clean up East Germany and bring together the two German states, and hopes that rich West Germany will be able to handle this.

Legal experts from both countries agree to allow criminals to be extradited from West to East Germany and vice versa. Each side is also fundamentally willing to transfer criminal matters to the other. No criminal should be able in future to escape responsibility.

The Round Table in East Berlin calls for appointment of a commissioner for foreigners, as the increase in xenophobia is becoming a cause for concern.

Fifteen thousand of the formerly 38,000-man strong East German border guard troop were dismissed by the end of January, according to their chief, Major General Dieter Teichmann; only 25,000 people will serve as border guards from now on.

Sales of the Berlin Wall are well under way throughout the world. »Several large Japanese firms have made offers, the Goethe Institute in Munich wants to buy four segments, and the famous English auction house, Sotheby's, is showing increased interest,« reports the Limex foreign trade firm, which is responsible for Wall sales. The company says the material, which has sentimental value, is currently selling for top prices of 500,000 marks per segment.

Saturday, February 17

The wave of emigrants to West Germany continues unabated. Since the beginning of the year, nearly 89,000 East Germans have gone West. Most of them claim to have no hope that East Germany will experience rapid economic recovery. In the entire previous year, 343,854 people moved from East to West Germany.

At a congress in Berlin, the Independent Women's Organization agrees to an electoral alliance with the Green Party. The association calls for the drafting of a social welfare charter in case of rapid German unification, since women are most likely to be affected by the process of economic restructuring.

The traditional Saturday demonstrations in Plauen (Vogtland) continue to be well-attended. Today, 15,000 people gather to demand rapid monetary union and German unity. In Leipzig, 20,000 respond to an SPD call for an election rally with West German guest speakers, and in Magdeburg, Democratic Awakening presents its program to an audience of 3,000.

Sunday, February 18

The chairman of the German Social Union (DSU) of East Germany, Hans-Wilhelm Ebeling, advocates adoption of the West German constitution, the Basic Law, following parliamentary elections on March

18.»Instead of drafting a new constitution ourselves, which the Round Table is just now attempting, we should adopt the one that has proven itself very well for forty years in the other part of our fatherland.«

According to the chairman of Democratic Awakening, Wolfgang Schnur, the Round Table in East Berlin has already »failed politically.« He says the democratic movement has not understood how to »recognize the real areas of concern to the people of the country.«

After decades in which public discussion was suppressed, a »Gay Union in East Germany« (SVD) is founded in Leipzig to better represent the interests of homosexual men in society.

Monday, February 19

At its 13th session, the Round Table expressly opposes the annexation of redefined East German states by West Germany as provided for in Article 23 of the Basic Law. The body ratifies a motion on this subject by the Initiative for Peace and Human Rights by an overwhelming majority (under Article 23, Saxony or Thuringia, for example, could simply declare on their own that they were joining the jurisdiction of the Basic Law). The Round Table also rejects NATO membership for the future united Germany.

Parties and political organizations at the Round Table agree to mount a fair election campaign. They state their intention to concentrate on presenting their own programs, goals, platforms and candidates and on objectively delineating their differences from other parties, organizations, initiatives, movements and persons. Any form of violence or aggressiveness is to be avoided.

The Round Table further decides to destroy all the Stasi's electronic data records by March 8. This is done to prevent their misuse and, in particular, to make rapid access to such data impossible, thus contributing to complete destruction of the structures of the former state security apparatus.

This Monday, loud demonstrations for German unity once again take place in numerous cities. In Leipzig, where only 20,000 people take to the streets, one banner announces, »Will exchange Luft* and Round

* *Refers to Minister of Economics Christa Luft.*

Table for Waigel* and DM.« In Halle, where the demonstration is most likely the last one before the elections, Lower Saxony's leader Ernst Albrecht (CDU) is a guest. He welcomes the planned monetary union and opposes devaluing savings. A rally in Karl-Marx-Stadt supports demands for restoring the city's original name, Chemnitz. The roughly 80,000 participants also shout »Germany, Germany!« and »Reds out, reds out!«

Tuesday, February 20

The People's Chamber adopts the long-awaited electoral law for the first free, secret elections on March 18. The law establishes that the new parliament will be elected for the period of four years and provides for 400 deputies (there have been 500 until now). There are no direct mandates; each voter has one vote, which he or she can cast for a party list or for a political association or joint list. The seats are calculated centrally for the entire Republic according to a proportional representation system. There are no minimum percentages (in West Germany, parties must garner more than 5% of the votes to enter parliament).

The German Federal Bank in Frankfurt announces that from now on, businesses in each German state may relocate or buy firms in their respective neighboring country without permission from West Germany. Until now, West German businesses required a permit from their central state bank.

Hang gliding is on the upswing in East Germany, and six new clubs have formed. In years past, hang gliders were subject to repressive measures, as they were suspected of trying to escape over the Berlin Wall. Because of this prohibition on flying in their own country, they were forced to enjoy their hobby secretly, mainly in Czechoslovakia.

* *Refers to West German Finance Minister Theo Waigel.*

Wednesday, February 21

The day after adopting an election law, parliament passes a law on parties and associations that allows East German parties to accept aid from West Germany for the current election campaign. It does prohibit parties from accepting gifts or other economic support from another country, but this article does not go into effect until January 1, 1991.

In the view of Soviet leader Mikhail Gorbachev, unification of the two Germanies is not just a German affair. In an interview with *Pravda*, the party newspaper, he calls for rapid assumption of the Two-Plus-Four Talks. »With all respect for their national rights, it can hardly be imagined, given the situation, that Germans would first agree among themselves and then allow others to bless decisions already made.«

The public prosecutor's office in East Berlin for the first time brings charges against former top politicians, including former SED Politburo member Harry Tisch and the former Chairman of the East German CDU, Gerald Götting. Investigations indicate that Tisch, longtime head of the FDGB labor union, independently diverted several million marks in solidarity payments to an FDJ youth festival, without the agreement of the organs in charge. In addition, he is alleged to have financed a generous hunting preserve, a house and private vacations out of union funds. Götting is also alleged to have bought a private house with party monies.

Thursday, February 22

As German unification draws nearer, the question of reparations for German destruction in World War II becomes acute for the West German government, as numerous foreign media are demanding such compensation. West Germany has hitherto rejected such claims, referring to the London Debt Agreement of 1953, under which Bonn promised the three Western powers and 30 other countries (not including the East Bloc) to pay off German foreign debt from the prewar period and the war years. In exchange, the parties put off reparation claims until after conclusion of a peace treaty. West Germany, which unlike East Germany saw itself as the legal successor to the Hitler Reich, had paid around two billion marks in reparations by the time of the 1953 London Agreement. East German reparations to the Soviet Union are estimated at between 65 and 100 billion marks. West German historian Arno Peters made headlines when he calculated that the West German government owes East Germany 727.1 billion marks – 74.3 billion in principal, plus interest since 1953.

Two thirds (67%) of West Germans acknowledge East Germany's moral claim to economic aid from the West. However, in a survey, 58% opposed the amount of the requested »solidarity contribution« of 15 billion marks. Thirty-eight percent consider the amount justified, and 5% feel this request for 10 to 15 billion marks is in fact too modest. A third of the respondents reject an East German moral claim to economic aid.

By the end of this month, all district offices of the former Ministry for State Security are to be closed down, according to an announcement by the head of the responsible government commission, Günter Eichhorn. He says the offices in the Schwerin district have already been closed. Roughly 68% of the employees of the former Stasi headquarters in East Berlin have been laid off, and 600 to 700 more are dismissed each day.

Friday, February 23

The Round Table working group on security approves a government proposal that the Main Department of Intelligence, responsible for foreign espionage, be allowed to dissolve itself without supervision by June 30, so as not to endanger people outside the country.

The transformation of public property into private businesses is to be first attempted with ten selected enterprises, according to the East German Ministry of Economics. Meanwhile, there have been roughly 1,300 applications for return of private businesses that were forcibly nationalized in 1972.

The German Bundeswehr Union and the Union of Professional Soldiers in East Germany plan to work together in the future in order to counteract old hostilities. A meeting for this purpose takes place in Strausberg, outside Berlin, between Admiral Theodor Hoffmann (PDS), the Defense Minister; Colonel Rolf Wenzel, Chairman of the German Bundeswehr Union; and the Chairman of the Union of Professional Soldiers in East Germany, Lieutenant Colonel Eckhardt Nickel.

Alliance 90, the alliance of civic movements, names its top candidates for the parliamentary elections: Jens Reich (New Forum), Wolfgang Ullmann (intended for the office of Prime Minister) and Konrad Weiß (both of Democracy Now), and Marianne Birthler (Initiative for Peace and Human Rights). The Green Party, for its part, fields Vera Wollenberger and Vollrad Kuhn; its ally, the Independent Women's Organization, tops its list with Ina Merkel and Walfriede Schmitt.

In the evening, East German television broadcasts the first ad for the elections on March 18. It is an ad for the Liberal Democratic Party (LDP) containing excerpts from speeches by West German politicians Otto Graf Lambsdorff and Hans-Dietrich Genscher (FDP) and an appeal for a social market economy.

Saturday, February 24

The Social Democrats choose their manager, Ibrahim Böhme, as party Chairman. This makes him both their top candidate and a candidate for Prime Minister in the March 18 parliamentary elections. Böhme expressly takes responsibility for his past membership in the SED. He says that, while he has a different view of parties today, he did not meet only »scoundrels and careerists« in the SED, and the Social Democrats must be prepared for personal reconciliation with former SED members. The Party Congress resolves to admit only those SED members who left the party before October 7, 1989.

Ex-Chancellor Willy Brandt is elected SPD Honorary Chairman, a position he already holds in the West German SPD. Speaking before a campaign rally of roughly 60,000 Leipzig residents, Brandt says that »what belongs together should now be allowed to sensibly grow together.« He thus plainly disagrees with the party leadership in Bonn, which views the unification process with greater skepticism.

At the start of a PDS Party Congress in Berlin, Gregor Gysi states that his party supports »East German independence in the unification process.« He says the Round Table should continue to operate even after the March 18 elections, as it has proven its ability to resolve problems.

Sunday, February 25

Prime Minister Hans Modrow will take the PDS into the elections as their top candidate, a decision he announces to the first PDS Party Congress. The roughly 600 delegates give the popular Prime Minister a rousing ovation and elect him honorary chairman.

The Chairman of the SPD, Ibrahim Böhme, extends his respect to Modrow's candidacy at the head of the PDS. He says Modrow is »a good candidate, but unfortunately in the wrong party.« Böhme calls it inconceivable that he could offer Modrow a position in an SPD-led cabinet after the March 18 elections.

In East Berlin, Lothar de Maizière, Chairman of the CDU, is nominated the party's top candidate for the elections.

At an electoral congress in East Berlin, 200 United Left (VL) delegates decide that the VL and the Marxist party The Carnations will form an »Action Alliance of the United Left« for the March 18 elections. The Alliance primarily targets those who support a sovereign East Germany.

More than 50,000 people demonstrate this evening at Lustgarten square in East Berlin for a sovereign East Germany and against dismantling of the social welfare system. Participants carry East German flags and banners saying »Don't let yourselves be fooled« and »Think of us children – we're the people too!« PDS Chairman Gregor Gysi voices opposition to an »annexation« of East Germany in which political, economic and social rights would be undermined. He calls for reform and change in both German states.

Monday, February 26

A published bill to reform the tax laws provides for radical tax cuts. Corporate income taxes would sink from a current maximum of 95% to 50%. Double taxation would be avoided in distributing profits. Taxes on board of directors' fees would be lowered from 65% to 30%, and the wealth tax from 2.5% to 1%.

The government announces introduction of unemployment benefits, which will pay up to 70% of the past 12 months' salary. The exact number of unemployed remains unknown, as the offices in charge are just being established.

The 14th session of the Round Table considers the problem of culture, demanding a law on cultural obligations for East Germany and saying that orienting culture entirely according to market criteria violates the public's right of free access to culture. The delegates also approve reform of the East German military. Defense Minister Theodor Hoffmann explains that, by year's end, the border guards will be separated from the National People's Army and placed under the jurisdiction of the Ministry of the Interior; also, NVA soldiers will from now on be permitted to engage in political organization and activity outside their service.

Some 15,000 to 20,000 people take part in the Monday demonstration in Leipzig. This time, instead of hand-painted posters, there are mainly commercially produced banners reading, »Not the SED, not the SPD – freedom instead of socialism.« The audience cheers mainly speakers from the right wing of the political spectrum who call for rapid German unification; Greens and Social Democrats who advocate a gradual coming together are whistled down.

Tuesday, February 27

The German Conference of Cities estimates there will be 1.5 to 2 million immigrants to West Germany in 1990, 600,000 to 700,000 of them from East Germany. The organization's Vice-President, Herbert Schmalstieg, says he fears this will cause serious conflicts on the housing market between immigrants and native West Germans seeking a place to live. »This is dynamite that greatly endangers social peace,« he says.

More than two thirds of all West Germans oppose letting in additional immigrants from East Germany. Sixty-eight percent support a cessation of such immigration, while only 28% advocate free entry. A survey shows that the originally positive attitude towards East German immigrants has clearly changed; half of all West Germans now believe that former East Germans enjoy unfair advantages in West Germany. The First Minister of Baden-Württemberg, Lothar Späth, calls in this context for private and government returnee bonuses for East German immigrants.

Israel hopes to establish diplomatic relations with East Germany in the near future. After signing a protocol on resumption of relations with Poland, Foreign Minister Moshe Arens tells journalists in Warsaw that East Berlin has signaled its willingness to go ahead with this.

Wednesday, February 28

Members of the National People's Army with long terms of service have no chance of being accepted into the Bundeswehr, according to West German Defense Minister Gerhard Stoltenberg (CDU). He says he has »serious reservations« about taking on former career or regular NVA soldiers who served in the middle or upper echelons. As grounds for this caution, he mentions security concerns due to the NVA's communist orientation until last fall.

The East German SPD dismisses a PDS (former SED) offer of partnership with the SPD. »We condemn any PDS attempt to polish up its damaged reputation through a ›partnership relationship with the SPD‹,« declares SPD manager Stephan Hilsberg in East Berlin.

According to the new party law, all parties and political associations must register with the President of the parliament regardless of whether they are participating in the upcoming elections or not. Of 38 parties and political associations, 35 have been registered.

March 1990

Thursday, March 1

To create capitalist labor conditions, nationalized businesses, facilities and combines are to be turned into corporations, according to a regulation adopted by the Council of Ministers that obligates all nationalized enterprises to transform themselves into companies, limited liability corporations (GmbH) or stock corporations (AG). A Trusteeship Agency is created for this purpose under the authority of the Council of Ministers.

The government further approves a draft law on the right of establishment, which allows foreign firms – formerly permitted only representation – to establish their own branches on the territory of East Germany for the purpose of economic activity.

The Minister of Social Welfare of North Rhine-Westphalia, Hermann Heinemann, demands rapid aid for East Germany. East Berlin must offer its residents a »bonus for staying« if the flood of emigrants from East to West is to be checked. The SPD politician strongly opposes the suggestion that East German immigrants should be paid bonuses for returning home. »If we pay such bonuses, even more people will come in order to get the money «

Chancellor Helmut Kohl is received enthusiastically by 200,000 people this afternoon in Karl-Marx-Stadt, where he calls for rapid economic and monetary union of the two Germanies. The CDU chairman again rejects requests for billions in immediate aid, saying he refuses to invest billions in a bankrupt system. It is much more important to introduce the West German mark, he maintains, but economic reforms are unavoidable if that is to be done.

Friday, March 2

In the words of an East German expert, investment of roughly 700 billion marks would be necessary to make the economy broadly »competitive and ecologically acceptable.«

According to West German Economics Minister Helmut Haussmann, private capital should bear the lion's share of the modernization of East Germany's outdated means of production.

CSU Chairman Theo Waigel believes concern over the economic effects of German unification is uncalled for. He is »deeply convinced that we can do it« and that it will even cost less »than many post-war tasks.«

Sects in East Germany are »strongly on the rise. Government and church are in despair over this development, smuggled in from the West, and see no way of dealing with it,« reports Dominican priest Klaus Funke, commissioner on sects in the Berlin diocese, in Hildesheim. He points out that a prevailing lack of orientation and a major vacuum in political, religious and social life are »just what [the sects] are looking for.«

Uwe Lehmann-Brauns, spokesman for culture in the Berlin CDU, speaks out against the »immortalization« of representatives of socialism on East German street signs. He proposes restoring in their entirety the East Berlin street names in use before the Nazi period.

Saturday, March 3

The Berlin Conference of Bishops sends out an urgent call to all Catholics to take political responsibility by participating in the elections. In a joint statement on the upcoming elections, the Catholic bishops and suffragans recommend voting for whoever »is most likely to guarantee you a true new beginning! Support those who want to bring to society that which is important to us as Christians! Help those who, in your opinion, have the strength to build a free, democratic polity governed by the rule of law! Ensure that under no circumstances do we get the old power structures back!«

Walter Wallmann, the leader of the West German state of Hesse, calls on West Germans to refrain from »hoarding« East German products. He says it makes him sad that more and more West Germans seem to be stocking up on subsidized basic foods in East Germany: »This only worsens existing supply bottlenecks in the other part of Germany.«

Rainer Kirsch (55) is elected the new Chairman of the reformed East German Society of Authors. His deputies are Joachim Walther and Bernd Jentzsch, and the Honorary Chairman by acclamation is Stefan Heym. Participants in an Extraordinary Congress of the Society in East Berlin advocate a greatly reformed East Germany and adopt a new statute, under which the Society describes itself as a »democratic, independent, non-partisan, non-profit organization of authors.«

Sunday, March 4

According to Helmut Fröhlich, Chairman of the Interhotels, East Germany is short of 85,000 hotel beds. »Interhotel GDR« currently has a bed capacity of 16,500 in only 13 towns, says Fröhlich at the International Tourism Fair in West Berlin; this meets neither international standards nor the special requirements of the incipient unification process.

Artists symbolically occupy the Palace of the Republic in East Berlin, headquarters of the parliament. This peaceful action is organized by East Berlin theater people who are active in an initiative called »November 4«; their aim is to create a center of alternative and experimental art in the prestigious building.

Monday, March 5

The inter-German preparatory commission of experts laying the groundwork for economic and monetary union meets privately in Bonn to discuss further modalities.

Bonn must provide 1.8 billion marks in integration assistance for 100,000 East German immigrants – money that could support 200,000 unemployed East Germans, according to West German Labor Minister Norbert Blum. He demands a change in existing laws.

At the 15th session of the Round Table, a social charter is adopted; also on the agenda are issues of equal rights for men and women, education, and youth.

The four major West German publishing companies, Springer, Gruner & Jahr, Burda and Bauer, begin to sell newspapers and magazines in East Germany at East German prices. They offer a total of 73 publications, not all of which come from the four major houses.

Tuesday, March 6

An East German government delegation, including the ministers without portfolio, meets with leaders in Moscow to coordinate the further progress of German unification. Both sides call for a »responsible, gradual growing together,« as part of which the western border of Poland must be accepted under international law.

SPD chief Ibrahim Böhme declares that his party would not want to govern alone, even if it were to receive an absolute majority in the elections. However, he is not yet willing to commit himself to possible coalition partners.

East and West Berlin will form their first joint administrative units, establishing two so-called directorates that will be staffed by civil servants from the West Berlin Senat and employees of the East Berlin Magistrat. The Mayors of West and East Berlin, Walter Momper (SPD) and Christian Hartenhauer (PDS), approve this arrangement during their first meeting in West Berlin.

Wednesday, March 7

Numerous laws are passed at the last session of the People's Chamber, the parliament, before the March 18 elections, including a new assembly law, a law on the purchase of publicly-owned buildings, and a law on the establishment of private enterprises.

Environmental activists from East and West meet for the first time as a group to launch an inter-German Green Table. Twenty-two delegates represent nature preservation societies, science, the economy and ministries from East and West Germany. Matthias Platzeck of the East German Green Party informs the delegates about initial joint decisions. The group demands that environmental protection be anchored in a new German constitution and calls for immediate establishment of a national parks program. It also opposes nuclear energy.

According to the Union of German Criminal Investigators (BDK), 14,000 suspected shoplifters were arrested in West Berlin in January and February. The number of apprehended shoplifters in two months is thus already equal to one third of the number in all of 1989. Roughly 40% of the suspects came from East Germany and East Berlin, while another 30% were mainly from Poland.

Thursday, March 8

In a unified Germany, East German women want abortion to continue to be available on demand during the first three months of pregnancy. On International Women's Day, Uta Röth of the Independent Women's Organization reports that all delegates of other East German parties at the Round Table have also called for retention of this arrangement. The government must also continue to subsidize education and day care.

The government relieves all »unofficial employees« (informers) of the former Ministry for State Security, the Stasi, of their responsibilities and their duty of secrecy. Some 109,000 people formerly utilized by the Stasi are thus forbidden to participate in further »conspiratorial activity.«

Of the 33,121 former employees of the Stasi headquarters in East Berlin, 29,300, or 88% of the staff, have been dismissed. Roughly 2,300 employees have been taken on by the border guards. The responsible citizens' committee reports to the Round Table that Stasi district offices in East Berlin have thus been largely dissolved.

In line with the most recent disarmament agreements, East Germany begins dismantling its medium-range SS-23 missiles. A spokesperson for the Defense Ministry confirms in the newspaper *Neues Deutschland* that all of the National People's Army's SS-23s will be destroyed by November. According to the Defense Ministry, East Germany possesses 24 of this type of missile, including four launchers, four transport vehicles, and the necessary security facilities.

Friday, March 9

Two weeks after the deadline for registration, the East German electoral commission officially announces that 24 parties, associations and joint lists will be running in the first free, general, equal, direct and secret elections in East Germany on March 18. The spectrum ranges from the Alternative Youth List to the major political parties to the German Beer Drinkers' Union.

In a campaign appearance in Rostock, Chancellor Kohl calls upon citizens to vote »all Communist bosses« out of office on March 18. Besides a sea of black-red-golden flags, a cheering crowd, and cries of »Germany!« and »Helmut!,« there is also massive protest by opponents of unification, and eggs and firecrackers are thrown. Kohl calls out to the crowd, »Don't let the rabble bother you!«

At the rally, Rainer Eppelmann, a leader of the Democratic Awakening party, brings greetings from his »unwell friend, Wolfgang Schnur.« Eppelmann defends Schnur against accusations in the press that he served as an informer for the Stasi; he says Schnur worked as a lawyer for years trying to help people victimized by the Stasi.

Thousands of German Federal flags are sent from Bonn during the election campaign in East Germany.
(photo by Frank Darchinger)

An »East German Farmers' Association« is formed by 630,000 farmers. At the first Farmers' Congress in 33 years, in Suhl, Thuringia, the roughly 900 delegates agree to thus rename the former »Association for Mutual Farmers' Aid.«

Saturday, March 10

Wolfgang Schnur, Chairman of Democratic Awakening, denies allegations that he worked for the Stasi. Schnur, in an East Berlin hospital suffering from circulatory problems, says these are »the peak of a campaign against me that was begun long ago.«

Only 10,000 people come to the Reichstag building in West Berlin to hear American evangelist Billy Graham speak. The itinerant Baptist preacher voices his hope that a spiritual revival can emanate from Germany. The purpose, he says, is to see that the walls between God and man fall, now that the inter-German Wall is gone.

In these closing days of the election campaign, dozens of rallies take place at which West German politicians are the main speakers.

Sunday, March 11

At an election rally in Magdeburg, Oskar Lafontaine, the SPD's candidate for Chancellor, advocates resolving East Germany's pressing social problems rather than arguing about constitutional articles. Speaking to an audience of 10,000 to 15,000, he calls for rapid creation of a new system of social benefits and retirement insurance. To the applause of the crowd, Lafontaine underscores his view that the Federal government should invest money in East Germany rather than spending it on immigrants to West Germany.

Some 2,000 people demonstrate on Berlin's Alexanderplatz square for the creation of a new, democratic society and against »throwing everything overboard« in the process of rapid unification. The rally is organized by a number of left-wing parties and groups, including the United Left, the Carnations, the KPD (West German Communist Party) and the PDS.

Ten thousand opponents of nuclear energy from both parts of Germany demonstrate peacefully at the site of a planned nuclear energy plant at Stendal (in the Magdeburg district).

Monday, March 12

The Round Table meets in East Berlin for its sixteenth and final session. Its 17 working groups take stock, acknowledging that the tasks they set themselves have essentially been completed. The Round Table assured effective public supervision of the government in the past months and at the same time submitted numerous draft laws.

A plebiscite on a new East German constitution is proposed for June 17; for this purpose, a draft constitution drawn up by a Round Table working group is to be made public and opened for discussion in April. The new parliament is advised to investigate its delegates for prior Stasi connections.

An initial viewing of the Stasi files cannot dispel allegations that Wolfgang Schnur, the chairman of Democratic Awakening, was a Stasi informer. With a special permit from the Prosecutor General's office, Minister Rainer Eppelmann and Schnur's attourney spent three hours going through the secret files on the DA chairman.

In the view of Klaus Wettig, an SPD delegate to the European Parliament, the East German economy will collapse within a year if no steps are taken to bring the two Germanies together.

More than 10,000 requests for acceptance into the Bundeswehr forces have been received from NVA soldiers since the fall of the Wall. The NVA has lost roughly two divisions of reservists through emigration to West Germany.

The very last Monday demonstration is held in Leipzig, and more than 50,000 people turn out to bid farewell to an event that has made their city famous beyond the country's borders. From the balconies of the opera house, the initiators lament the fact that the political culture of the past autumn, marked by dialogue and tolerance, has been lost during the campaign.

Tuesday, March 13

During the night, four young East Berliners beat up an East German border guard for trying to check their IDs on the way to West Berlin. When the soldier asked for ID, they sprayed paint in his face and beat him with an iron chain. This morning, the Defense Ministry points out that the border still may only be crossed at the crossing points set up for this purpose.

At another meeting of experts to prepare for monetary union, representatives of East and West Germany agree that the future economic community will be supported by a social compact. No concrete date has yet been set for introduction of the West German D-Mark, nor have exchange rates been fixed.

A special commission of the East German Council of Ministers announces that its investigations indicate 15 million marks in hard currency were spent in 1989 alone for privileges for certain groups of people. Of this amount, six to eight million were used to supply the private Politburo community in Wandlitz.

Wednesday, March 14

The four victorious World War II powers and the two German states begin joint negotiations in Bonn on the process of German unification.

DA Chairman Wolfgang Schnur announces his resignation. On East German television this evening, Schnur's former Stasi handler talks about Schnur's activities as an informer, saying Schnur provided mainly information on Church groups, peace groups, and environmental and human rights initiatives. According to the ex-Stasi officer, Schnur had risen to become a »top informant« with the cover name of »Dr. Schirmer.« An independent investigative commission in Rostock says 33 file folders of information on Schnur are stored in the former Stasi headquarters there. Schnur refuses to receive his party comrade Rainer Eppelmann; instead, surprisingly enough, he summons Prime Minister Modrow to his sick bed. During the visit, he not only asks Modrow for protection for his family, who live in Rostock and East Berlin, but apparently also apologizes for attacks on Modrow by his party in recent days, in which he was accused of being the »initiator of a smear campaign.«

Thursday, March 15

East Berlin Pastor Rainer Eppelmann is chosen the new Chairman of the Democratic Awakening party. At the same time, the delegates expel Schnur for his behavior.

After the final meeting of the Modrow government, government spokesman Wolfgang Meyer says the overall balance is positive. He points to the initiation of constructive steps toward reform – for example, the adoption of the party and election law – with which the »Government of National Responsibility« strengthened the democratization process.

The media supervisory council permits the reintroduction of advertising on East German radio.

Friday, March 16

A new all-German constitution, decided upon by plebiscite, is a necessary prerequisite to German unity, according to SPD Presidium member Gerhard Schröder. Schröder believes that for East Germany simply to join West Germany under Article 23 of the Basic Law would be unfortunate, as this would deprive West Germans of the opportunity to voice their opinion on this significant issue.

The Hesse State Office for the Protection of the Constitution announces that it had received and passed on extensive information more than a month ago regarding connections between the Stasi and the former Chairman of Democratic Awakening, Wolfgang Schnur, and East German CDU General Secretary Martin Kirchner.

The campaign in East Germany is officially over at 9 p.m. The West German Ministry for Inter-German Relations in Bonn announces that a total of at least 7.5 million DM have flowed into the East from the West German party-sponsored foundations, 4.5 million from the CDU alone, which distributed 20 million flyers, 5 million election newspapers, 2.5 million calendars, and half a million posters. On the other hand, the East German Greens received nothing.

Saturday, March 17

The Ministry of Finance and Prices issues a statement announcing that the sale of unused state-owned buildings and real estate at replacement value is now possible. This can also be taken advantage of by property owners whose homes are located on state-owned land.

Prominent East and West Germans call for a plebiscite on the question whether East Germany should continue to exist or be united with West Germany. They say such a fundamental issue cannot be decided by governments alone.

West German Minister of Labor Norbert Blüm criticizes the cautious attitude of the SPD under Oskar Lafontaine and Johannes Rau on the German question. He claims the »Social Democrats' betrayal of solidarity at this level« disgusts him, and adds, »If the Saarländers had been treated in 1957 the way Lafontaine is now treating East Germans, the Saarland would not yet be a member of the Federal Republic today.«

Sunday, March 18

The CDU is the clear winner of the first democratic elections in East Germany, gaining 40.6% of the votes. The Union ends up in first place in 12 of 15 districts. It is especially successful in the southern districts, where the Alliance for Germany garners 60% to 62% of the votes, and in small towns. The SPD achieves only a surprisingly weak second place, with 21.8%. It wins only a few large cities and Berlin, where the Alliance receives only 22%. The PDS achieves a total of 16.3%, enjoying its best result of 30% in Berlin. The civil rights groups, whose representatives were popular spokespeople of the civic movements in the weeks of the autumn Wende, all remain under 5%. Participation is pegged at 93%.

Willy Brandt comments that German unity has been elected, »rapidly and with no ifs, ands or buts.« »I hope that we can travel with real money by the summer,« declares Lothar de Maizière, the top CDU candidate, on election eve. Wolfgang Ullmann of Democracy Now is bitterly disappointed. On East German television, author Stefan Heym's comment on the outcome is, »There will be no more East Germany. It will be nothing but a footnote in world history.«